Margaret Atwood's

The Edible Woman

Text by
Jeffrey M. Lilburn
(B.A., McGill University; M.A., The University of Western Ontario)

Illustrations by
Karen Pica

 Research & Education Association
Dr. M. Fogiel, Director

MAXnotes® for
THE EDIBLE WOMAN

Printed in the United States of America

Library of Congress Catalog Card Number 98-66039

International Standard Book Number 0-87891-231-2

MAXnotes® is a registered trademark of
Research & Education Association, Piscataway, New Jersey 08854

What **MAXnotes®** Will Do for You

This book is intended to help you absorb the essential contents and features of Margaret Atwood's *The Edible Woman* and to help you gain a thorough understanding of the work. The book has been designed to do this more quickly and effectively than any other study guide.

For best results, this **MAXnotes** book should be used as a companion to the actual work, not instead of it. The interaction between the two will greatly benefit you.

To help you in your studies, this book presents the most up-to-date interpretations of every section of the actual work, followed by questions and fully explained answers that will enable you to analyze the material critically. The questions also will help you to test your understanding of the work and will prepare you for discussions and exams.

Meaningful illustrations are included to further enhance your understanding and enjoyment of the literary work. The illustrations are designed to place you into the mood and spirit of the work's settings.

The **MAXnotes** also include summaries, character lists, explanations of plot, and section-by-section analyses. A biography of the author and discussion of the work's historical context will help you put this literary piece into the proper perspective of what is taking place.

The use of this study guide will save you the hours of preparation time that would ordinarily be required to arrive at a complete grasp of this work of literature. You will be well-prepared for classroom discussions, homework, and exams. The guidelines that are included for writing papers and reports on various topics will prepare you for any added work which may be assigned.

The **MAXnotes** will take your grades "to the max."

Dr. Max Fogiel
Program Director

Contents

Each chapter includes List of Characters, Summary, Analysis, Study Questions and Answers, and Suggested Essay Topics.

MAXnotes® are simply the best – but don't just take our word for it...

"... I have told every bookstore in the area to carry your MAXnotes. They are the only notes I recommend to my students. There is no comparison between MAXnotes and all other notes ..."
– High School Teacher & Reading Specialist, Arlington High School, Arlington, MA

"... I discovered the MAXnotes when a friend loaned me her copy of the *MAXnotes for Romeo and Juliet*. The book really helped me understand the story. Please send me a list of stores in my area that carry the MAXnotes. I would like to use more of them ..."
– Student, San Marino, CA

"... The two MAXnotes titles that I have used have been very, very useful in helping me understand the subject matter reviewed. Thank you for creating the MAXnotes series ..."
– Student, Morrisville, PA

A Glance at Some of the Characters

Marian McAlpin

Ainsley Tewce

Peter

Duncan

Clara

Trevor

Fish

Mrs. Grot

SECTION ONE

Introduction

The Life and Work of Margaret Atwood

Few writers have equalled the success Margaret Atwood has enjoyed since her first collection of poetry was published in 1961. One of the leading Canadian writers of her generation, Atwood has garnered international acclaim as a poet, novelist, short story writer, critic, and author of children's books. She has now published over 30 books of verse and prose and translations of her works have appeared in over 20 languages. A favourite among academics and the general reading public alike, Atwood has been honoured with numerous literary awards and nominations. She has won the Governor General's Award twice (for the book of poems *The Circle Game* in 1966 and for her novel *The Handmaid's Tale* in 1986) and has been short-listed for the prestigious Booker Prize three times. The last time was in 1996 for her novel *Alias Grace*.

Atwood was born in Ottawa, Ontario, in 1939. The years of her childhood and early adolescence were divided between the cities of Toronto, Ottawa, and Sault Ste. Marie, and the bushes of Northern Ontario and Quebec. Although she developed her literary interests early in life, beginning to write when she was still a student in high school, Frank Davey (1984) writes that it was as an undergraduate at the University of Toronto's Victoria College, where she studied under the highly respected literary critic Northrop Frye, that Atwood discovered and developed an interest in Canadian literature. This interest sparked a career that helped change the literary landscape in Canada and led countless other students of literature to discover for themselves the Canadian literary tradition.

By 1961, Atwood had not only obtained her B.A. in Honours

English, she had also won the E. J. Pratt medal for her first published book of poems, *Double Persephone*. In 1962, she received
an M.A. from Radcliffe College and began doctoral studies at
Harvard. The years that followed, documented by Davey (1984),
Carrington (1985), and VanSpanckeren and Castro (1988), brought
much change and many moves. She interrupted her studies in 1963
and returned to Toronto to work for a market research company.
Then, after spending a year in Vancouver lecturing at the University of British Columbia and writing what would become her first
published novel, *The Edible Woman*, Atwood returned to Harvard.
However, she left once again to accept teaching positions at Sir
George Williams University in Montreal and the University of Al-
berta in Edmonton. During the next four to five years, Atwood
published five more volumes of poems, including *The Animals in
That Country* and *The Journals of Susanna Moodie*, and her
second novel, *Surfacing*.

During the 70s and 80s, Atwood continued to publish regularly, received numerous honourary degrees, and held positions at
universities across North America and abroad. Some of her most
successful novels were published during this time, including *Lady
Oracle* (1976), *Cat's Eye* (1988), and *The Handmaid's Tale* (1985).
The latter was adapted for the screen in 1990. During the 1990s,
Atwood has published two novels—*The Robber Bride* and *Alias
Grace*—two collections of short stories and one book of poems. She
currently resides in Toronto with her husband, novelist Graeme
Gibson.

Historical Background

Along with novelists such as Mordecai Richler, Michael
Ondaatje, Margaret Lawrence, and Robertson Davies, Margaret
Atwood is one of the most respected and successful writers ever to
emerge from Canada. But Atwood's popularity is not limited by bor-
ders: she is an internationally renowned poet and novelist known
for addressing serious issues and social problems with humour and
wit. Respected by feminists for her exploration of gender politics,
Atwood also explores humanity's relationship to nature and often
parodies many of our social and cultural conventions.

Atwood is often described by critics as a writer concerned with the search for identity. Her first three novels, for example, have been described as Romances and Gothic Romances in which the narrator must search for her identity in a dark and threatening world (Carrington, 1985). But for Atwood, the search for personal identity is often paralleled by the search for a national one. When she began publishing in the 1960s, Canadian writers were considered "freaks of nature" (Atwood, *Great Unexpectations*, 1988), inferior to, or pale imitations of writers from England or the United States. In 1970, she published the collection of poems *The Journals of Susanna Moodie* in which she examines Canadians' attitudes towards their own country. Two years later, she published *Survival: A Thematic Guide to Canadian Literature*, a nonfictional critical analysis of Canadian literature, and has continued to address Canadian subjects and themes in her poetry and prose. The relationship between English and French cultures in Canada is a major issue, as is Canada's relationship to the United States. The latter plays a major role in Atwood's second novel, the immensely successful *Surfacing*. In it, the American culture of consumerism and violence, often criticized in Atwood's writing, is described by the narrator as "the disease. . . spreading up from the south."

The influence of American culture in Canada is also addressed in Atwood's first novel (Marian's job at a market research company links her to consumer culture, as does her relationship with Peter, a soon-to-be successful lawyer and caricature of the ideal male), but it is fused with problems relating to gender politics. The Americanized culture of consumerism is a male world. The question asked by Marian at the beginning of the novel, "What could I expect to turn into at Seymour Surveys?" is representative of the questions many women were asking in the mid-1960s. Throughout the novel, Marian attempts to define her identity in a world where the models, plastered on advertisements and decorating the covers of magazines, have all been manufactured by men. Expected to conform to a societal ideal of femininity, Marian struggles to break free of what she initially views as her inevitable fate.

The early reviews of *The Edible Woman* were mixed; some praised Atwood's ironic satire, others found reason to fault (Carrington, 1985). In fact, over the years, certain critics have maintained that Atwood's true talent is to be found in her poetry, not in her novels. Nevertheless, *The Edible Woman* established Atwood as a writer of fiction and is now a highly respected work that has been the subject of much scholarly debate. Funny, perceptive, and thoroughly entertaining, *The Edible Woman* is a remarkable first novel by one of North America's finest contemporary authors.

Master List of Characters

Marian McAlpin—*main character, narrator, a young single woman, university educated, currently working for a market research company.*

Ainsley Tewce—*Marian's roommate, also single and university educated, currently working as a tester of defective electric toothbrushes.*

Duncan—*an English Literature graduate student.*

Trevor and Fish—*Duncan's roommates, also graduate students of English Literature.*

Peter—*Marian's boyfriend/fiancé, he is in his articling year as a lawyer.*

Clara—*Marian's friend from high school and college.*

Joe—*Clara's husband.*

Arthur and Elaine—*Clara and Joe's children.*

Len Slank—*a college friend of Marian and Clara's.*

Trigger—*a friend of Peter's; he gets married early in the novel.*

Marian and Ainsley's landlady—*unnamed.*

Landlady's daughter—*unnamed.*

Marian's office colleagues:

Mrs. Withers—*the company's dietician.*

Mrs. Grot—*accounting clerk.*

Mrs. Bogue—*head of Marian's department.*

Emmy, Lucy, Millie—*collectively, the three office virgins (a term coined by Ainsley).*

Summary of the Novel

The Edible Woman tells the story of Marian McAlpin, a young single woman who works for a market research company. Unable to foresee a fulfilling career within the company, she begins to worry about her future and about what she might become. One night, she comes to the unsettling realization that her relationship with her boyfriend, Peter, is more serious than she thought it to be. She tries to evade the matter by running away. Yet, when Peter proposes marriage that very night, Marian accepts. She had always assumed that she would get married, and Peter, she thinks, is an ideal choice: he is a lawyer and is bound to be successful. Similarly, Peter feels that marriage will aid his career.

Despite her engagement, Marian continues to see Duncan, the aimless graduate student of English Literature, whom she met while conducting door-to-door interviews for an ad campaign. The day after Peter proposes, they run into each other at a laundromat where they talk and share an unexpected intimate moment in the form of a kiss. Marian thinks the event is unrelated to Peter.

As she watches Peter cut his steak at dinner one night, Marian suddenly visualizes the diagram of a planned cow, outlining all the different cuts of meat. She is unable to finish the steak on her own plate and soon discovers that she can no longer eat meat that has any indication of bone, tendon, or fibre. Before long, the refusal spreads to other foods, leaving her unable to eat many of the things she used to enjoy. She begins to fear that she may not be normal but her married friend, Clara, assures her that the eating problem is simply a symptom of bridal nerves and that she will soon get over it.

As the wedding date approaches, Peter decides to throw a party. He enjoys displaying Marian and hints that she might want to get her hair done and buy a new dress. She complies by buying a red sequined thing that is, she thinks, not quite her. As she walks home, hair heavily scented and every strand glued in place, she thinks of herself as a cake: something to be carefully iced and ornamented. At the party, while Peter prepares to take a group photo, Marian realizes that she must escape. She finds Duncan and the two spend the night together in a hotel. The next morning, she is unable to eat a thing and has no choice but to confront her problems.

According to Duncan, Marian's problems are all in her mind: she has invented her "own personal cul-de-sac" and will have to think her own way out.

Later that afternoon Marian bakes a cake shaped and decorated into the likeness of a woman. When Peter arrives, she accuses him of trying to assimilate her and offers the cake as a substitute. He leaves quickly, without eating, and Marian begins picking at the cake herself. By the final chapter, Marian has called off the wedding and is eating regularly. Duncan tells her that she is "back to so-called reality"—a "consumer" once again. Marian then watches as Duncan eats the rest of the cake.

Estimated Reading Time

The Edible Woman is divided into three parts and thirty-one chapters. The major shift that occurs between parts is a change in the narrative voice. Parts One and Three are told in a first-person voice, while Part Two is narrated from a third-person perspective. Chapter length remains relatively consistent throughout the novel, as does the narrative style and general level of difficulty. Atwood's prose is clear and easy to understand on a first reading and, as a result, readers may be tempted to read too quickly. But be warned! Margaret Atwood's writing is intricately structured and contains many hidden complexities. Close readers will be rewarded.

Expect to spend about one hour for every three or four chapters. Below is a suggested reading schedule that follows the breakdown used for this study guide and includes estimated reading times for each section:

Chapters	1 - 4:	45 minutes
Chapters	5 - 8:	70 minutes
Chapters	9 - 12:	70 minutes
Chapters	13 - 16:	75 minutes
Chapters	17 - 19:	1 hour
Chapters	20 - 22:	1 hour
Chapters	23 - 25:	45 minutes
Chapters	26 - 29:	75 minutes
Chapters	30 - 31:	15 minutes

As with any good book, a second reading will greatly increase your understanding and enjoyment of this literary work.

SECTION TWO

The Edible Woman

Chapters 1-4

New Characters:

Marian McAlpin: *main character, narrator*

Ainsley Tewce: *Marian's roommate*

Peter: *Marian's boyfriend, he is in his articling year as a lawyer*

Clara: *Marian's friend from high school and college*

Joe: *Clara's husband*

Arthur and Elaine: *Clara and Joe's children*

Len Slank: *college friend of Marian and Clara*

Trigger: *friend of Peter*

Marian and Ainsley's landlady: *unnamed*

Landlady's daughter: *unnamed*

Marian's office colleagues:

Mrs. Withers: *dietician*

Mrs. Grot: *accounting clerk*

Mrs. Bogue: *head of Marian's department*

Emmy, Lucy, Millie: *collectively, the three office virgins*

Summary

It is morning and Marian and her roommate, Ainsley, are preparing for the last work day before Labour Day weekend. Marian works for Seymour Surveys, a market research company, where she revises questionnaires. It is a good job, better than most she thinks, yet she can't help envying Ainsley her job as tester of defective electric toothbrushes. Marian thinks of her job as the kind of position one is expected to have after earning a B.A.; Ainsley's is unusual and more temporary. Hung over from a party she attended the night before, Ainsley tells Marian that her evening was so dull that she had to console herself by getting drunk. Marian suddenly realizes that she is running late, quickly eats a bowl of cereal and heads for the bus stop. On her way out, she is stopped by the landlady who questions her about the smoke that was emanating from the girls' apartment the night before. Marian explains that it was just the pork chops but is still given words of warning to pass along to Ainsley.

Marian is 45 minutes late when she arrives at work and is almost immediately recruited by Mrs. Withers, the dietician, to taste-test new flavours of canned rice pudding. When she gets back to her desk, she contemplates her position with the company. She has the impression that she is being groomed for something higher up, but does not know what. Marian's office, all female, is the link between the men upstairs and the machines below and does not provide her with any visibly attainable goals. Her uneasiness is amplified when she receives a visit from Mrs. Grot of Accounting, who tells her that she is now eligible for the mandatory pension plan. Marian reluctantly signs the necessary forms, but feels as though she has put her name to a magic document that binds her to an unavoidable, distant future. She welcomes the ten-thirty coffee break and joins Emmy, Lucy, and Millie (collectively dubbed the three "office virgins" by Ainsley) at the restaurant across the street. Ainsley, whose office is nearby, joins them. Marian complains to her friends about the obligatory pension plan, but is merely told that she will soon get over it.

After lunch, an unexpected problem arises concerning an upcoming beer study and Marian is asked if she would be available to conduct pretest interviews over the weekend. Feeling that her

lateness that morning gives her supervisor leverage, she agrees to do the interviews. Soon afterwards, she receives a call from Peter, her boyfriend. He is upset because his last unmarried friend, Trigger, is getting married. As a result, the plans Marian and Peter had for dinner that evening are cancelled. Marian is disappointed but then gets a call from her married friend, Clara, who invites her to dinner. Marian immediately accepts but then, fearing that she will be expected to act as entertainer and confidante, asks if she can bring Ainsley.

Upon their arrival, Marian and Ainsley are greeted by Joe, Clara's husband. It isn't long before everyone's attention is focused on Elaine, one of Clara and Joe's two children. Marian feels that her role for the evening is that of blotter: she must absorb some of Clara's boredom. She must also be careful not to mention anything that might remind Clara of her inertia. Clara asks Marian if she is still seeing Peter but it is Ainsley who answers, saying that Marian is still seeing Peter and has, in fact, been monopolized by him. Clara then mentions that Len Slank, an old college friend, is back in town. Ainsley appears interested and asks about this old friend but is told that he is horrible with women and not somebody to get mixed up with; attention is again diverted to one of the children, this time to Arthur. He has hidden the contents of his diaper and Joe is sent searching. Marian remembers how Clara had not planned to have kids so early in life. The first pregnancy had been a surprise, the second was "greeted. . . with dismay" but, now that a third baby is on the way, Clara seems to have subsided into a "grim but inert fatalism." Marian and Ainsley leave soon after dinner.

Analysis

In these first four chapters, Atwood introduces many of the central themes and issues that will be explored throughout the rest of the novel. Of central concern is Marian's uncertainty about who she is and who she fears she might become. She is in her mid-twenties, has completed her university education, and is now struggling to find her identity in a male dominated business world that does not provide her with any visible means of advancement or fulfillment. She feels trapped in her menial job revising market survey questionnaires and, after signing the obligatory pension plan

forms, feels manipulated and unable to influence the development of her own life. The magic document bearing her signature, held in a cabinet by the "men upstairs," seemingly binds her to a future where a preformed self awaits.

Yet, Marian's uneasiness about the direction her life is taking is accompanied by passive compliance. At work, she turns the convoluted and subtle prose of market study questionnaires into simple questions that can be easily understood and digested by the average mass consumer. The results of such questionnaires are then used to develop new ways of reaching, influencing, and manipulating the general public. She makes similar adjustments to herself in order to meet social expectations. She wears the high-heeled shoes that are expected of her—even though they force her to walk sideways when descending the stairs of her own home—and allows the men upstairs to dictate how she spends her time over a long holiday weekend. Like Millie, who tells her that she will soon get over her problems with the pension plan, Marian, too, has learned to adjust to things.

Marian's willingness to shape herself according to the expectations of the workplace anticipates later scenes in the novel where she again shapes herself in order to please Peter. According to Ainsley, Marian has been monopolized by her boyfriend, a term that suggests control and ownership and that is generally associated with goods and commercial activity, not personal relationships. But, in these four chapters, there is already evidence that individuals' personal lives are not lived outside of the realm of consumer culture. Marian is personally involved in the world of advertising and consumption. She works for a market research company and is participating in the development of a new ad campaign for Moose Beer—a campaign designed to make the average beer-drinker feel a "mystical identity with a plaid-jacketed sportsman shown in the pictures." Buying this brand of beer, the ad implicitly claims, will transform the buyer into the societal ideal of rugged masculinity. One of the questions raised by this advertisement is whether it is celebrating the image of the "real man" or constructing it. It is a question that recurs throughout Atwood's novel.

When Marian asks, "What. . . could I expect to turn into at Seymour Surveys?" it is as though she has already conceded that her identity will be shaped by the images and options presented to her. In fact, the answer to her question is suggested through her colleagues at work. The three office virgins, all trapped in the same office and all waiting to be rescued by a husband, represent one of Marian's possible fates. Similarly, her married friend, Clara, resigned to what Marian herself calls a "grim but inert fatalism," represents another—or perhaps just a later stage of the same one.

Another significant detail in these early chapters is Marian's preoccupation with food. At breakfast, she worries that she will be hungry again long before lunch. She stops for peanuts on her way to work and then, once there, is recruited to taste test new flavours of canned pudding. There is also the morning coffee break and dinner at Clara and Joe's that evening. In fact, much of the novel's first part is structured around food, and readers may want to begin thinking about how the consumption of food relates to other forms of consumption.

Study Questions

1. What is Marian's job?

2. Why does she envy Ainsley her job as a tester of defective electric toothbrushes?

3. Where do Marian and Ainsley live?

4. Describe Marian's relationship to Ainsley.

5. What does Marian look at on her way to work?

6. Why is Marian unhappy with her company's mandatory pension plan?

7. What is Ainsley's nickname for Marian's colleagues, Emmy, Lucy, and Millie?

8. Why is Peter upset about his friend Trigger's marriage?

9. When Marian visits her friend Clara, what does she think her role will be for the evening?

10. What does Ainsley think of Marian's relationship to Peter?

Answers

1. Marian works for Seymour Surveys, a market research company. She revises questionnaires.

2. She thinks Ainsley is lucky because her job is more temporary and unusual.

3. They live on the top floor of a large house in one of the older and more genteel districts of town.

4. They are roommates but do not have very much in common. They met just before they moved in together. Before that Ainsley was a friend of a friend.

5. She likes to look at the advertisements in the bus on her way to work.

6. Marian feels as though the pension plan binds her to an unavoidable future where a preformed self awaits.

7. Ainsley's nickname for them is the three "office virgins."

8. Trigger was the last of Peter's unmarried friends. When their other friends had gotten married, Peter and Trigger had "clutched each other like drowning men."

9. She thinks her role will be that of blotter. That is, she will have to absorb some of Clara's boredom.

10. Ainsley thinks that Marian has been monopolized by Peter.

Suggested Essay Topics

1. Marian is concerned about the direction her life will take if she remains employed at Seymour Surveys. Discuss her reaction to this concern.

2. In this section of the novel, Marian mentions and describes several of the women who work in her office. How do they relate to Marian's present situation? Discuss.

Chapters 5-8

New Characters:

Duncan: *an English Literature graduate student*

Trevor and Fish: *Duncan's roommates, also graduate students*

Summary

As Marian and Ainsley walk through the dusk towards the subway, Ainsley wonders how Clara can stand such an existence. She
feels that Clara allows herself to be treated like a thing while Joe
does all the work. At the very least, Ainsley suggests, Clara could
return to school and finish her degree. These criticisms of her
friend's current lifestyle lead Marian to recall how, after Clara's first
child was born, she had considered her absence from school as
temporary. Lately, however, she had started to think of herself, bit-
terly, as "just a housewife."

When they get home, Marian calls Len Slank and the two make
plans to meet the following evening for drinks. During their conversation, Len asks Marian about the new man she is seeing and
whether or not it is serious. Marian assures Len that her relationship with Peter is not at all serious. As soon as she is off the phone
Ainsley again inquires about Len. She then tells Marian that she
has something important to tell her: she wants to have a baby.
Marian initially interprets this as meaning that Ainsley is getting
married. This surprises Marian because Ainsley has always been
decidedly anti-marriage. Ainsley assures Marian that she has
absolutely no intention of getting married. In fact, she believes that
families like Clara and Joe's do not provide an ideal situation for a
child: the child's mother-image and father-image will be confused.
The thing that ruins families, Ainsley argues, is the husband. It is
a child Ainsley wants, not a man.

Marian is baffled but does not know how to justify her opposition to Ainsley's plan. When she asks Ainsley why it is she has
suddenly decided that she wants to have a baby, her roommate
tells her that every woman should have one because it "fulfils your
deepest femininity." "Don't you feel you need a sense of purpose?"

she asks Marian. In response, Marian considers all the time and energy that will be required to pack and move all of the furniture. She always knew that their living arrangement was not permanent but, now that it was threatened, it began to take on a "desirable stability."

According to Marian, Ainsley has decided to have an illegitimate child and bring it up by herself. Society being the way it is, Marian thinks the child will suffer. Ainsley challenges this view and asks how society will ever change if certain individuals in it do not make an effort to better it. After a few moments of silence, Marian finally asks about the father. Ainsley admits that she has not yet chosen a father but says that he will have to be someone fairly good-looking with decent heredity. He will also have to be cooperative and not make a fuss about marrying her. Marian goes to her room thinking about ways to stop her friend. She then becomes resigned, wondering whether Ainsley's personal life is any of her business. She decides that she will "simply have to adjust to the situation."

The next morning, Saturday, Marian gets up and prepares for a day of interviewing. She breakfasts alone and traces several possible routes on a city map. After breakfast, Marian travels to the chosen neighbourhood and rings the day's first doorbell. She explains to the woman who answers that she is conducting a market research survey about beer and asks to speak to her husband. The woman invites Marian inside where she is greeted by a tall man in a black coat who tells her that "the propagation of drink and drunkenness to excess is. . . a sin against the Lord." Marian tries to explain that her company is not actually involved with selling beer but is told that it does not make a difference. It's the same thing, he tells her: "Those who are not with me are against me, saith the Lord." The next interviewee, already drinking a beer when Marian rings the doorbell, answers the survey questions but then lurches towards her wearing a half-drunken leer. Marian hands him the "Temperance" pamphlets given to her by the preacher and flees.

She completes four more interviews and enters an apartment building at the end of the street. The first door she tries is answered by a cadaverously thin and melancholy looking figure wearing only a pair of khaki pants. Believing the man to be much younger than he actually is, Marian asks to speak to his father. He tells her that

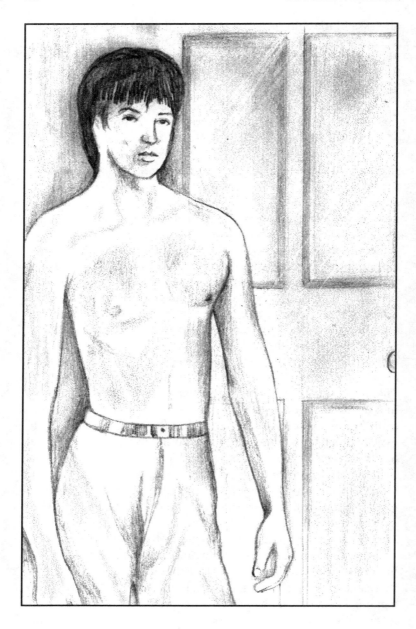

he is 26 and invites her in. (Although Marian does not yet know his name, the young man is Duncan.) The apartment is furnished with three huge easy chairs and a bookcase that extends the length of the living room wall. Nearly everything is covered with books and papers. Not wanting to mess up his or his roommates' papers, Duncan leads Marian into his bedroom. They sit down on his bed and Marian begins the interview. Duncan's answers are imaginative and offbeat and cause Marian to imagine the reactions of the women who will later read them. She also begins to suspect that her subject might be "tottering on an emotional brink."

Near the end of the interview, Marian asks Duncan how each of the five phrases she has read to him applies to beer. He tells her that he would not know—he drinks only scotch. At the beginning of the interview he had stated that he drank an average of seven to ten bottles of beer per week. Now, he explains that he was bored and merely wanted to talk to someone. He then claims, confidently, that Marian enjoyed his answers. Marian is annoyed and can't decide whether she should get up and leave or admit that he is right. Just then the front door opens and Duncan's two roommates walk in. A voice from another room asks Duncan if he would like a beer. Caught in a lie, he admits that he simply did not want to complete the interview. Marian gets up and is about to leave when Duncan asks her why she has such a crummy job. She tells him that everyone has to eat and then, borrowing Ainsley's favourite retort, asks: "What else can you do with a B.A. these days?"

After completing her interviews, Marian returns home and takes a bath. She then goes to Peter's. When she arrives, Peter is still in the shower. She takes the groceries she has brought into the kitchen and then strolls into the bedroom and looks over Peter's various material possessions. There is a bookcase filled with law books and detective novels and a pegboard holding his collection of weapons and cameras.

Peter, wearing only a towel, eventually emerges from the shower and invites Marian into the bathroom. He then leads her into the bathtub where they make love. Marian does not think this a good idea, preferring the bed, but does not object. She feels that she needs to be sympathetic because Peter will be depressed over Trigger's marriage. She thinks of the two other "unfortunate

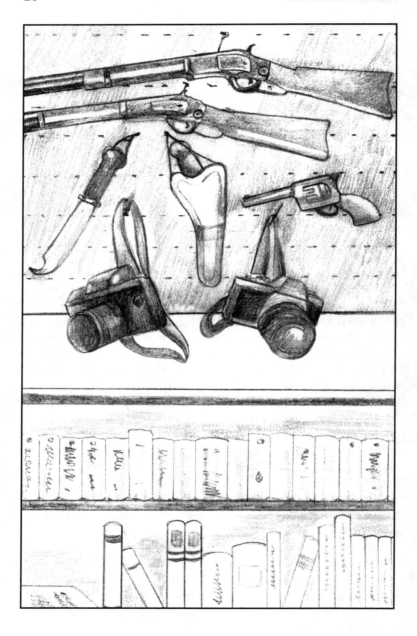

marriages" of Peter's friends. After the first one, Peter had led her onto the sheepskin rug in the bedroom; the second time, he brought her and a scratchy blanket into a field. Marian thinks the bathtub is part of the same pattern: it is Peter's attempt to assert youthfulness and spontaneity. She also thinks that Peter likes these occasions because he read about them somewhere, possibly in an outdoorsy magazine or murder mystery novel. She notices Peter's smell: he always smells of soap, a smell Marian associates with dentist's chairs and medicine. She then considers his face—a face Clara has described as good-looking. Marian thinks of Peter as "ordinariness raised to perfection" and sometimes wishes she would find a reassuring irregularity, "something the touch could fix on instead of gliding over." She then remembers their first meeting. Peter had liked her independence and saw her as the kind of girl who would not try to take over his life. Marian had to learn how to adjust to Peter's moods but this, she believes, is true with any man. As she lies in the tub thinking and reminiscing, Peter suddenly whispers into her ear and bites her shoulder. Marian reciprocates and turns on the cold water.

Later that evening, Marian and Peter go out to meet Len. During dinner, Peter had gone on about the wedding and how Trigger had been sucked into the "domestic void." He then thanked Marian for being so understanding and sensible. They join Len at the Park Plaza, a rooftop hotel bar in the city. Len talks of England, where he lived for a while, and tells how the women there are always after you to marry them: "You've got to hit and run," he tells Peter. A few moments later, Ainsley makes a surprise appearance. Knowing that Len likes his women young, she has altered her appearance accordingly. Len beams at her, excited that Marian's roommate is so young. Marian knows why Ainsley has come: Len is a potential candidate for her baby plan. As a result, she is uncertain whether she should give away Ainsley's game or participate in what amounts to fraud. She watches as Ainsley gives short, shy answers to Len's questions and, thinking it unethical for her to let Len be deceived, goes out on the patio to think. She wonders whether or not it is any of her business but worries that Ainsley may somehow retaliate if she says anything.

When Marian returns to the table, Peter and Len are deep in

conversation and barely notice her. Peter is telling Len a hunting story and Marian recalls how he had once told her that he never killed anything but vermin, crows, and groundhogs. But this story involved gory and bloody details about gutting a rabbit. She listens to Peter tell Len how funny it was and imagines the scene. She sees Peter standing with the friends she has never met, a rifle on his shoulder, their faces splashed with blood, and their mouths "wrenched with laughter." Wanting desperately to talk to Peter and to hear his normal voice she leans forward but he does not respond. She then discovers that she is crying and retreats to the bathroom. There, she continues to cry for several minutes without understanding why. Finally, Ainsley finds her and the two return to the table.

Peter and Len are now talking about the various methods of taking self-portraits. Len gives Marian a peculiar look that she does not immediately understand but soon realizes that he is trying to tell her something. His look, Marian believes, is meant to convey his belief that she is being purposely self-effacing and that her relationship with Peter is more serious than she had said it was. She thinks Len has misinterpreted. Suddenly, the panic that sent her crying to the bathroom returns. As the bar closes, Len invites them all over to his place for another drink. Peter accepts but, once outside, Marian lets go of Peter's arm and begins to run.

Analysis

Chapter 6 opens with Marian's description of a dream. In this dream, she watches as her body seemingly dissolves. Her feet ooze like "melting jelly" and the ends of her fingers turn transparent. She wakes up before getting the chance to see her face or understand what exactly is happening to her. She then goes on with her day. The association between this dream and Marian's fading sense of identity is obvious: uncertain about the direction her life is taking and feeling unable to alter or deviate from the options presented to her, Marian is less than secure with who she is and who she fears she is turning into. The factors contributing to Marian's perceived self-dissolution are addressed throughout Atwood's novel and will continue to be discussed throughout this volume.

The word "adjust" appears many times in *The Edible Woman.*

When Marian first learns of Ainsley's plan to have a child, she opposes the idea. But this opposition quickly turns to resignation, and Marian tells herself that she "will simply have to adjust to the situation." Similarly, Marian's entire relationship with Peter can be said to consist of a never-ending series of adjustments. Early in Marian and Peter's relationship, he tells her that one of the reasons he likes her is because he considers her to be "the kind of girl who wouldn't try to take over his life." Peter's early take on Marian turns out to be accurate. Not only does she not attempt to take over his life, she willingly allows her own to be taken over. She does so under the assumption that she has "to adjust to [Peter's] moods," something she believes to be true of all relationships with men. A pattern is set during the early stages of the courtship that continues to repeat itself throughout their relationship. The first time Marian goes to Peter's apartment, she allows herself to be "manipulated into the bedroom." On the day after Trigger's wedding, Marian allows Peter to lead her into his bathtub, even though she would clearly prefer the bed. She does not object because she feels she needs to sympathize with Peter's distress over Trigger. She goes along with Peter's "whim" and ends up thinking of herself as a lavatory fixture.

Marian's job at Seymour Surveys also leads her to compromise her true feelings. Despite her fear of being entrapped by the company's pension plan, Marian rushes to her employer's defense when one of her interviewees accuses Seymour Surveys of using her to advance their own "abominable" objectives. Marian attempts to silence the man by telling him that her company "doesn't have anything to do with selling the beer." Her accuser remains unconvinced and informs her that those who are not with the Lord are against him. For Marian, the implication of this line (religious connotations aside) is clear: by refusing to resist and take a stand against the company's exploitative business practices, she automatically implicates herself in their activities.

Unlike Marian, Duncan does not willingly adjust himself according to the desires of others. At the very least, he is aware of the external forces that are attempting to adjust him. To Marian, Duncan's behaviour is outside of what she considers to be normal. In fact, Duncan's answers to the beer questionnaire lead Marian to suspect that he might snap at any moment. She amuses herself by imagining the reactions of the ladies who read and compile the results; Duncan's answers would, Marian believes, provide the ladies with material for at least three coffee breaks. She then imagines what might happen if she was to feed Duncan's answer sheet to the IBM machine at the office. Such a thought implies that Duncan's responses are so outlandish that they would be unreadable by the machine. With this passage, Atwood demonstrates how Marian, like the ladies to whom she refers, has already developed a firm sense of what is and is not normal. Answers that don't meet the machine's programmed expectations must, Marian seems to believe, be unworthy of serious study or consideration. Marian thus reveals something of an aversion to thoughts and behaviours that do not fit into a standardized norm. Given these attitudes towards what is normal, Marian's choice of a boyfriend—a man she thinks of as "ordinariness raised to perfection, like the youngish well-groomed faces of cigarette ads"—becomes a little more understandable and a little more troubling.

In the pivotal scene at the Park Plaza bar, Marian experiences two sudden attacks of panic without understanding what is causing them. The first instance occurs after listening to Peter tell Len his blood- and gut-filled hunting story. Marian realizes that the wet drops on the table in front of her are her own tears and suddenly becomes aware that "something inside [her had] started to dash about in dithering mazes of panic." Her understanding grows after she deciphers the meaning of the "peculiar look" Len throws her way. Len, she decides, must think that her relationship with Peter is more serious than she had said it was. Although Marian thinks that Len is mistaken, she does, for a moment, see her present position from his perspective: she was allowing Peter to treat her as a "stage prop," a "two-dimensional outline," and was being "self-effacing on purpose." It is after considering these possibilities and, more importantly, after considering what they imply, that Marian, in a renewed state of panic, runs away. Especially interesting in this scene is the fact that Marian's body reacts to the external events happening around her before she is even aware that something is wrong. This apparent split or detachment from her own feelings anticipates other significant happenings later in the novel.

Study Questions

1. Why does Ainsley criticize Clara's lifestyle?

2. What reason does Ainsley give for wanting to have a baby?

3. What does Marian decide to do about her friend's sudden decision to have a child?

4. What is Marian's first impression of Duncan?

5. How did Marian meet Peter?

6. Why does Peter choose the bathtub (according to Marian)?

7. Why does Ainsley show up at the bar dressed to look much younger than she actually is?

8. What does Marian decide to do about Ainsley's use of deception?

9. How does Marian interpret the look Len gives her in the bar?

10. Why does Marian run away? What (or who) is she running from?

Answers

1. Ainsley thinks that Clara allows herself to be treated like a thing. She thinks that she should *do* something.

2. Ainsley thinks every woman should have a baby because "it fulfils your deepest femininity."

3. Marian initially tries to think of a way to stop Ainsley but then becomes resigned, thinking that it isn't any of her business. She decides that she will simply have to "adjust to the situation."

4. When Marian first sees Duncan she thinks that he is about 15. She is also struck by his thinness (he is described as "cadaverously thin" and as an "emaciated figure" whose ribs stick out) and melancholy eyes.

5. Marian met Peter at a garden party following her graduation. He was a friend of a friend. They began seeing each other over the summer and he soon became a "pleasant habit."

6. Marian thinks that the bathtub lovemaking fits into the same pattern that began after two other "unfortunate marriages." She thinks that Peter is trying to assert his youthfulness and spontaneity by revolting against the stale doom he associates with marriage.

7. Ainsley knows that Len likes his women young and hopes that he will be a suitable candidate for her baby plan.

8. Marian thinks that it is unethical of her to let Len be deceived but wonders what she can do and whether it is any of her business. She is also afraid that Ainsley may somehow retaliate if she ruins her plans.

9. Marian suspects that Len gives her a look because he thinks that she is being purposely self-effacing and that her relationship with Peter is more serious than she had said.

10. There is no simple answer to this question. Marian herself may not know why she begins to run.

Suggested Essay Topics

1. Marian opposes Ainsley's decision to have a child. Why? Discuss the differences between their attitudes towards men and marriage.

2. Duncan does not allow himself to be "adjusted" the way Marian does. Is this statement true? Depending on your answer, discuss his importance in the novel.

Chapters 9-12

Summary

Surprised by Marian's sudden sprint, Peter, Len, and Ainsley do not immediately react. Peter is the first to yell after Marian but turns back to get his car rather than give chase on foot. He soon catches up to her but Marian, threatened by the fact that he chose to enclose himself in the armour of his car, turns into a gateway and runs up the gravel driveway of an old house. As she approaches the house, the front door opens and Marian leaps into some hedges and crosses the lawn. Her flight is interrupted when she comes up against a brick wall. Hearing Len quickly approaching behind her, Marian attempts to climb over the wall. She manages to get on top of it but then begins to sway dizzily and falls. She is caught by Peter who sped around to the back of the house in his car. He is annoyed by her behaviour but does not make a fuss.

Marian, relieved to hear Peter's "normal voice" again, slides willingly into the car. They arrive at Len's apartment and ascend the stairs in "decorous couples." Inside, Peter begins to fiddle with a couple of Len's cameras and Marian, feeling deflated, wishes she could be alone with Peter so he could forgive her. She sits on Len's bed sipping a cognac and becomes entranced by the space between the bed and the wall. It would be quiet down there, she thinks, and quickly glances around the room. She wedges herself sideways between the bed and the wall but finds it uncomfortable. She then pushes the bed out a little and slides all the way under. Now completely out of view, Marian is glad not to have to sit up there in the hot glare of the room. However, her initial satisfaction is quickly replaced with discomfort and she wishes the others would hurry up and discover that she is missing.

After a few minutes under the bed, Marian is unable to remember what reasons led her there in the first place. She begins to feel resentment towards Peter for letting her remain down there while he moves about freely. This resentment starts her thinking about the past four months: they had deluded themselves into thinking that they were static. They had avoided talking about the future because they figured they were not really involved. But now

something in her had decided that they were involved. This, she thinks, is the reason for her earlier breakdown and flight: she was evading reality. She thinks that now, this very moment, she will have to face reality and decide what she wants to do.

Meanwhile, someone sits on the bed and squashes Marian against the floor. She gives out a cry and is discovered. Peter tells her to come out but Marian finds that she is stuck. The bed is lifted and Marian gets up, covered with dust, to face their questions. She tells them that she went under the bed because it was quieter. Peter takes her arm and prepares to leave but Marian refuses to go back with him. Once again she runs off on her own. Outside, Marian feels better: she had broken out, she had acted. A decision had been made and, after that embarrassing display, there could be no reconciliation with Peter. She walks towards a main street intending to catch a bus but Peter pulls up ahead of her. Believing that she is now no longer involved, she sees no reason to run. He asks if she would allow him to drive her home and, since it was about to rain, Marian permits herself to be led into the car. He asks her, angrily, what all the evening's nonsense has been about. Marian, however, is convinced that her behaviour was not nonsense and does not want to discuss it. Each thinks the other behaved badly and Peter accuses Marian of rejecting her femininity. Marian thinks that Peter was just plain rude.

By the time Peter pulls away heavy rain has started to fall. Driving too fast on the already slick roads, he loses control of the car and crashes into a hedge. Neither Peter nor Marian is injured in the accident but Marian bounces off the dashboard and accuses Peter of trying to "get us all killed." Commenting on her own exclamation, Marian says she must have been thinking of herself as plural. Peter merely laughs at Marian's reaction—and at the damage done to the property—and drives off.

They soon arrive in front of Marian's apartment and Peter suggests that she wait a few minutes for the rain to stop. He leans towards her to remove a piece of dust from her hair and Marian goes limp. They end up sitting with their foreheads pressed together, gazing into each others' eyes. After a few minutes, Marian tells Peter that she does not know what she was doing earlier. In response, Peter strokes Marian's hair in what she considers a

somewhat patronizing fashion and asks her to marry him. A flash of lightning illuminates the inside of the car, and Marian sees herself mirrored in Peter's eyes. Her answer remains unknown.

When she wakes up the next morning, Marian feels as though the inside of her head has been scooped out "like a cantaloupe." She finds Ainsley in the kitchen and asks if she got home okay. Ainsley tells her that she took a taxi from Len's place and explains that acting dumb and scared with Len was necessary at this stage of her game. Marian then announces that she and Peter are engaged. Ainsley is not surprised by the news but suggests that she and Peter get married in the States since it is so much easier to get a divorce there. She is of the opinion that Marian does not really know Peter. Marian explains that, subconsciously, she probably wanted to marry Peter all along.

While preparing her breakfast, Marian notices that Ainsley is busily studying a calendar, planning her strategy with Len. Marian again feels uneasy about her roommate's plans but justifies her inaction by telling herself that Ainsley's use of Len could in no way damage him. Wishing to hear a more positive reaction to her engagement than the one she received from Ainsley, Marian calls Clara. Her friend is pleased, but the announcement does not produce the excitement Marian was hoping it would.

After breakfast, Peter drops by unexpectedly to discuss the events of the night before. He greets Ainsley with an enthusiastic "Well!" and sounds, Marian thinks, as though he has "just bought a shiny new car." He tells Marian that although he had not planned what happened last night, perhaps he had intended it "without knowing it." He also tells her that their marriage will surely aid his career. Watching him speak, Marian begins to see Peter in a new light: he was no longer the reckless bachelor but a "rescuer from chaos" and a "provider of stability." She imagines an invisible hand wiping away her signature at Seymour Surveys. Peter then asks when she would like to get married. Her reply, spoken in a voice she barely recognizes, is: "I'd rather have you decide that."

Peter leaves early and Marian is left with the feeling of having nothing to do. She decides to spend the evening at the laundromat. She takes the bus and, as in Chapter 1, entertains herself by looking at the advertisements. One of the ads features a young woman skipping about in a girdle and leaves Marian feeling "slightly scandalized." She wonders to whom the image of the "lithe young woman" depicted in the ad is supposed to appeal. When she gets to the laundromat she discovers that she has forgotten her soap. A young man next to her offers her some of his and recognizes Marian as the woman who gave him the beer interview. The young man (Duncan—Marian still does not know his name) tells her that he did not immediately recognize her without her "official shell." He then tells her that he comes to the laundromat a lot because he finds it soothing to watch the washers. He also mentions his fondness for ironing—it gives him something to do with his hands. Duncan continues to talk and Marian gets the sense that he is talking to himself.

Eventually, Duncan reveals that he and his roommates are all graduate students in English Literature. Marian pretends to find this interesting, and Duncan explains that it is just like anything else: it's something you get stuck in and then you can't get out. He tells her there's no good reason for doing it and that everything has already been done. Marian suggests that he might be happier doing something else but Duncan explains that once you've gone this far, you are simply not fit for anything else. He also discusses his home life and explains that he cannot move out because his roommates take good care of him.

Marian thinks all this "liquid confessing" is something that she could never do—she sees it as a risk. She considers offering Duncan some kind of consolation but thinks that there is something about him that suggests an unnaturally old man far beyond consolation. He tells her that he knows she is admiring his "febrility" and warns her that he tends to evoke the Florence Nightingale in women. He then tells her to be careful—she might do something destructive. Hunger, he says, "is more basic than love" and "Florence Nightingale was a cannibal." Marian, not knowing what to think or of what she is being accused, gets up and empties her machine. They leave the laundromat at the same time and almost collide when they get outside. Standing face to face on the sidewalk, they spontaneously drop their bags and kiss. Afterwards, they pick up their bags and walk away in opposite directions.

In the final chapter of Part One, Marian contemplates the events of this long Labour Day weekend. It is Monday, Labour Day, and Marian now views her actions as "more sensible than [she] thought." She admits that the decision to marry Peter was sudden, but thinks that it was actually a good step to take. She'd always assumed that she would get married and have children—everybody does. Also, she thinks Peter is an ideal choice for a husband: he's attractive, bound to be successful, and neat. She still cannot account for the kiss with the man from the laundromat (Duncan) but decides that it must have been some kind of lapse. She dismisses the incident, telling herself that she does not even know his name and that it had nothing to do with Peter. In the last paragraph, Marian remains lying on her bed, gazing up at the ceiling. She feels as though she is on a raft, drifting. This is, presumably, the position she has been in for quite a while, reflecting on the events of the past four days.

Analysis

The first time that Marian runs away from Peter, she is surprised by her own spontaneous actions. She then begins to feel a sense of accomplishment and measures each passed lamp post as "distance-markers" on her course to independence. However, mixed in with the feeling of accomplishment is a sense of disappointment when Peter does not run after her. When she is finally caught, Marian is relieved to have her flight interrupted. Shortly afterwards, as the foursome arrive at Len's apartment, Marian's tone and perspective change yet again. She describes the scene as though she herself is an observer, not a participant: "we ascended the stairs in decorous couples." The description, tinged with the knowledge that individuals are taught and made to feel that you must be part of a pair to be whole, reads like a commentary on the socially constructed value attached to "coupledom." It suggests doubts about the widely accepted and advocated idea that to be a complete person requires two people.

Once inside the apartment, Marian's behaviour remains ambiguous. Alone under Len's bed, Marian initially finds the solitude pleasant. She finds it satisfying to be the only one who knows where she is. But it is not long before she begins to wish that the others would hurry up and notice that she is missing. She becomes upset with Peter because he is able to move about the room while she remains cramped under the bed. In short, Marian appears to be struggling with conflicting desires: she wants to flee, to be on her own, but part of her also wants to be found and to be with Peter. It is at this point that she begins to think of the past four months and realizes that she and Peter have been deluding themselves. She concludes that they are indeed involved and again runs off on her own.

After a short-lived resolution to find her own way home, Marian surrenders to Peter's arguments and allows herself to be placed into his car. To him, Marian's actions make no sense. In fact, he calls her behaviour "nonsense" and accuses her of "rejecting her femininity." What Marian is rejecting, of course, is Peter's definition of femininity and what that definition entails. Unfortunately for Marian, she too is confused by the predefined gender roles into which society expects women to fit. She disagrees with Peter's dismissal of her behaviour but then, considering how her behaviour might appear to others, thinks he might be right. Throughout the novel, Marian repeatedly moulds herself into what others—especially Peter—want and expect her to be.

Marian defends her actions, briefly, but then goes "limp" and concedes that she does not know what she was doing earlier. It is at this moment, when Marian is doubting her own beliefs, that Peter proposes marriage. Marian's immediate reaction to the proposal is to move away from Peter, in a sense repeating the movement acted out earlier during her two attempted flights. But this time she does not flee. Instead, she looks at the distorted reflection of herself mirrored in Peter's eyes. Her answer (withheld until the following chapter) implies that she sees and accepts his vision/version of herself. If this scene leaves any doubt about the repercussions of Marian's decision, the opening lines of the following chapter make clear the full implications of her passivity. When she wakes the next morning, she feels as though her mind is "as empty as though someone has scooped out the inside of [her] skull like a cantaloupe. . ."

Marian's and Peter's behaviour on the day after the proposal is equally revealing. Peter utters tired clichés about it being "time to settle down" and greets Ainsley with a tone that suggests he has "just bought a shiny new car." He also shares his thoughts on "choosing a wife," noting that he has always thought it important to find a "sensible girl." Similarly, Marian feels the "proprietary instinct" beginning to kick in and thinks of Peter as "an object" that belongs to her. She then astounds herself by abdicating all of the big decision-making responsibilities to Peter—and she does so in a "soft flannelly voice" she barely recognizes. Marian is even more astonished by the fact that she meant what she said. A short while ago she was, like the hunted evading its hunter, running through city streets and climbing brick walls to get away from Peter. Now, at the prospect of becoming his wife, she automatically assumes the attitudes and physical attributes expected of that role.

Later in the day, while preparing to spend the evening at the laundromat, Marian makes a joke about having cut Peter into little bits which she intends to dump in the ravine. The joke proves to be somewhat prophetic since it is at a ravine, later in the novel, that Marian finally faces her problems and makes the first serious steps towards regaining her independence and sense of self (by dumping Peter). The violence embedded in the joke is also significant. Earlier, Marian described Peter's glance towards her in a language that suggested the possibility of violence: Peter's "eyes narrowed as though he was taking aim." Elsewhere, his stare is described as "intent" and "faintly ominous." Such examples hint at a lingering feeling of vulnerability. Similarly, it is because Peter presses "murderously hard" on the accelerator that the car swerves out of control. Marian reacts to the incident by accusing him of trying to kill her. Even during an intimate moment in Peter's bathtub, Marian is reminded of his fondness for murder mysteries and imagines that he got the love-in-the-tub idea from one of the novels he has read. She then likens the bathtub to a coffin and associates their lovemaking with death. Together, these scenes appear to suggest that, in Marian's mind, union with Peter leads to death—not a literal death, but the death of a part of herself.

As Marian is riding on the bus on her way to the laundromat, we get a glimpse at how individuals' expectations and beliefs can be manufactured and manipulated. Marian occupies herself by looking at the advertisements, her favourite activity when using public transportation. At first, she does not know what to make of an ad featuring a young woman skipping about in a girdle; she thinks it strange to sell girdles by using an image that appeals mostly to men. She then realizes that the image might be a suggested self-image for women. Earlier, Marian had glanced at some magazine quizzes, the kind that claim to have all the answers on topics such as love, marriage, and sex. Both the girdle ad and the self-help questionnaires illustrate advertisers' strategic attempts to tell women what they should look like, what they should wear, and, ultimately, who they should be. Such ads help maintain a false and unrealistic sense of what is real and normal—a subject already discussed in the previous section and one which will come up again as Marian continues to question her own normality—and can account, at least in part, for Marian's feelings of self-doubt. They constitute, in effect, a major tool used to standardize expectations and impose social pressures.

In the final chapter of Part One, Marian decides that her decision to marry Peter was actually a good one—even though it is inconsistent with her "true personality." She thinks she has always assumed, ever since high school and college, that she would one day get married. It is significant that Marian associates these assumptions with school. Earlier, Marian spoke of the constraints that are imposed upon individuals and how, from a very early age, we learn to accept the rules that we had no part in making. In Marian's words, "you get adjusted to that at school." What is implied here is that we are forever subjected to someone else's conception of what is real and of what our lives should be. Duncan calls university the "braingrinder," a place where, after a while, differences (accents) are erased and "you don't sound as though you're from anywhere." While not an attack on education in general, these passages do add to the novel's criticism of an indoctrination process that sees individuals forced into an existing system of acceptable and predefined roles. Advertising's manipulations are thus only an extension of what goes on in other social arenas.

Finally, Marian's thoughts at the very end of this section do not bode well for her relationship with Peter or for herself. She thinks of her eventual marriage to Peter as though it is a business transaction. She criticizes Clara and Joe for not knowing how "to manage [or] run a well organized marriage" and believes that she and Peter will be able to "set up a very reasonable arrangement." Not once during these thoughts of marriage does the word love ever cross her mind. And not once does Marian appear excited or enthusiastic about her choice. She simply says: "I must get organized. I have a lot to do." After all, life "isn't run by principles but by adjustments." Or so Marian believes.

Study Questions

1. Describe Peter's, Len's, and Ainsley's reactions when Marian begins to run away from them.

2. What does Marian find so attractive about the dusty space beneath Len's bed?

3. Describe Marian's thoughts as she lies hidden beneath the bed.

4. Why does Marian run away yet again after Peter gets her up?

5. How does Peter react to the property damage he causes with his car?

6. What is Ainsley's reaction to Marian's engagement to Peter?

7. How do Marian and Peter view their engagement to each other?

8. Describe Duncan's fascination with laundromats. Why does he go there so often?

9. What are Duncan's thoughts on being a graduate student of English Literature?

10. Summarize Marian's thoughts in the last chapter of Part One. Is she being honest with herself? Is she trying to justify her actions somehow?

Answers

1. At first all three are astonished and do nothing. Peter and Len start after Marian but Peter turns back to get his car. When they finally catch up to her, Peter asks what the hell got into her. Len tells her that he did not think her the

hysterical type. The next morning, Ainsley tells Marian that she behaved like a "real idiot."

2. She thinks it would be quiet. Once underneath, she feels like she is underground, as though she had dug herself a private burrow away from the others "up there."

3. She begins to feel resentment towards Peter for letting her remain down there while he moves freely in the open. She also decides that her relationship with Peter is more serious than she had let herself believe. She decides that she will have to face reality.

4. After getting her out from under the bed, Peter acts superior and amused. He then assumes control by taking her arm. Marian describes her prevailing emotion as rage. Outside, Marian is not certain why she has been acting this way but decides that at least she has acted.

5. He laughs and then steps on the gas, causing even more damage by spinning his wheels.

6. Ainsley barely reacts at all. She is not surprised and merely offers some advice: she recommends they get married in the States since it is much easier to get a divorce there. She doesn't think Marian knows what she is doing.

7. The day after he pops the question, Peter shows up at Marian and Ainsley's apartment acting like he just bought a new car. He tells Marian that he is going to be much happier now that things are settled. He also thinks that being married will aid his career. Meanwhile, Marian is thinking of Peter as a "provider of stability" and "rescuer from chaos."

8. Duncan likes to watch washing machines because "you always know what to expect." Going to the laundromat is an escape for him, an escape from his apartment and his work.

9. Duncan says that words "are beginning to lose their meanings." He says that being a graduate student is like anything else: you get "stuck in it and you can't get out." He also says that there is no good reason for doing it and that everything has already been done. Of course, Duncan's parody of

graduate studies is only partially accurate. . . Does he truly believe what he is saying? Is being unfit "for anything else" seen as a good or bad thing?

10. Marian describes her sudden decision to marry Peter as a "good step to take." However, she can't quite "fit in" the kiss with the man at the laundromat. She thinks the incident is unrelated to Peter. Is this true? This chapter is the last one narrated in the first person until the very end of the novel. Considering the thoughts expressed here, is the shift in narrative point of view significant?

Suggested Essay Topics

1. Marian finds lots to think about while she is hidden under Len's bed. Why is she there? Why does she run away again? Why does she then allow Peter to drive her home? Discuss Marian's behaviour in this section of the novel.

2. Discuss the significance of Peter's use of the word "nonsense."

3. What is so important about a girdle ad seen on a city bus?

Chapters 13-16

Summary

Part Two of the novel marks a shift in narrative voice: whereas Marian narrated the first 12 chapters in the first person, the next 18 chapters are delivered in the third person. There is also a shift in time: two months have passed since Marian's engagement to Peter. Chapter 13 opens with a description of Marian sitting "list-lessly" at her office desk. She doodles while around her the rest of the office is in a turmoil. She used to feel a sense of participation in these minor excitements but ever since her engagement—and ever since she knew that she would not be there forever—she has viewed her surroundings with a certain amount of detachment. In fact, she discovers that she cannot get involved or interested even when she would like to.

Lunching out with Emmy, Lucy, and Millie, Marian is asked about Peter. She has been keeping her engagement a secret from her office friends but the question catches her off guard. Unable to resist, Marian smiles glowingly and announces that she and Peter are getting married. She then watches as the expressions around her turn from expectation to dismay. Momentary elation is followed by a series of remote and impersonal questions about the wedding. Finally Lucy asks: "How on earth did you ever catch him?" Marian looks away from their "pathetic and too-eager faces" and says that she does not know. Now that she has told them, she feels sorry for having raised their hopes without being able to produce a set of instructions for accomplishing the same.

After lunch, Peter calls Marian to cancel their dinner plans. The cancellation leads to a minor disagreement and Marian hangs up the phone feeling exhausted. Later in the afternoon she gets a call from Joe with news that Clara has finally had the baby (it was late). She tells him that she will visit Clara tomorrow. Marian had been putting off the visit because she felt unable to handle another evening spent "contemplating Clara's belly." Now that her friend was "deflating toward her normal size," Marian thinks that she will be able to talk to her more freely. She even buys flowers as a welcome-back gift for the real Clara.

As soon as she gets off the phone, Marian becomes acutely conscious of time and imagines it lifting her body out of the office towards the day in the future when she and Peter will marry. She senses that somewhere arrangements are being made, things are being taken care of. Meanwhile, she floats, "trusting [the current] to take her where she was going." Later in the afternoon, Mrs. Bogue reports that there has again been trouble with the "Underwear Man." The underwear man, Mrs. Bogue explains, is a man who poses as a Seymour representative and asks women dirty questions over the phone. Marian thinks that maybe the man is a victim of society, crazed into a frenzy by girdle advertisements. She is still thinking about him when she leaves work and, for a moment, believes that the underwear man could be Peter. Perhaps that was his true self, the secret identity that had been occupying her mind more and more lately.

When Marian gets home, Ainsley informs her that tonight is

the night for her plans with Len. Although two months have passed
since their first meeting, the image Ainsley constructed during their
first encounter was so pure and innocent that Len has taken things
extra slow. She tells Marian that she plans to invite Len up for coffee after their dinner date and let herself be backed into the bedroom. Marian agrees to go out for awhile and even lends Ainsley
her bedroom (which is neater than Ainsley's) for the good of the
plan. She decides to pass the time by going to a movie and, on her
way to the theatre, is again plagued by the thought that she should
warn Len. She then remembers the tacit agreement she and Ainsley
have had ever since her engagement: neither was to interfere with
the other's strategy.

Sitting in the movie theatre, Marian hears cracking noises coming from the seats beside her and discovers that the man from the
laundromat (she still does not know Duncan's name) is sitting two
places away. She is glad to see him but considers this an "irrational
gladness" and does not intend to speak to him. As she watches the
movie, a peculiar sensation enters her left hand: it wants to reach
over and touch Duncan's shoulder. She then hears a voice whis-
pering in her ear: "pumpkin seeds." She turns around but there
isn't anybody there. Thinking she may have imagined the incident,
Marian fears that she may be going insane. However, the bright
lights at the movie's end reveal a pile of shells on the ground where
Duncan had been sitting.

Upon her return home, Marian is greeted by her landlady. She
tells Marian that she heard a man mount the stairs earlier in the
evening and has not yet heard him come down. Marian assures
the landlady that whoever it was must have come down quietly
and tells her that she will talk to Ainsley about it in the morning.
Inside the apartment Marian discovers a man's tie wrapped around
the door to her room (Ainsley's signal that she is in bed with Len)
and reluctantly spends the night in Ainsley's cluttered bedroom.

The following afternoon, Marian goes to the hospital to visit
Clara. Having watched "the whole thing" Clara shares both her excitement and some of the "messy" details with her visitor. She tells
Marian that she ought to try it sometime. For Marian, having a baby
was something she had always planned to do eventually, but here,
in the hospital with Clara, the "possibility [seemed] suddenly much

too close." Clara congratulates Marian on her engagement to Peter and proceeds to share some of her attitudes towards her own
husband, Joe. She tells Marian that although she now knows that
Joe is not Jesus Christ, she still considers him to be "one of the minor
saints." Marian finds this attitude complacent and embarrassing.
She concludes that Clara is trying to give her some kind of oblique
advice and finds this even more embarrassing; Clara is the last person from whom Marian would seek guidance. When her visit is over,
Marian walks out of her friend's room feeling as though she has
escaped from something. She is glad that she is not Clara.

Walking through the hospital hallways, Marian goes over her
plans for the evening. Originally, she and Peter were to go out for
dinner. However, a surprise call from Duncan led her to change
these plans. He apologized for startling her at the movies and told
her that he needed her help: he needed her to bring him some ironing. Marian agreed to see him after work and cancelled her dinner
with Peter. She justifies her decision by telling herself that she could
see Peter any night and that this was an emergency.

Marian makes a quick stop at her apartment after work and
receives an update on Ainsley's progress with Len. She learns that
the landlady went out that morning and that Len was able to sneak
out unseen. She then departs with a bundle of clothes under her
arm. At Duncan's, Marian sits on the edge of his bed and watches
as he irons her clothes. When he is done, Duncan explains that
although he is not addicted to ironing, he sometimes goes on
binges. This one, he says, started when he dropped his term paper
in a puddle on the kitchen floor. He had to iron it and then started
ironing everything in the house that was clean. Then he had to do
laundry, which was why he was at the movies that night. He had
gotten bored watching the machines.

After a few minutes, Duncan asks for the blouse Marian is
wearing and hands her his dressing gown. Marian again watches
as he irons the "cloth [that] had been so recently next to her skin."
When he is done with the blouse, Duncan crawls onto the bed and
lies down next to where Marian is sitting. He wonders aloud how
anything ever gets done, complaining that the same actions, such
as writing term papers, are always repeated. It's like "a treadmill,"
he says. Marian is only half listening to what he is saying,

concentrating instead on his face and wondering how anyone that thin could remain alive. Duncan tugs her down beside him and puts his arms around her. Marian gets the impression that he is caressing his own dressing gown. She kisses him and tells him that she is engaged. That, Duncan tells her, is her problem. In fact, the news makes him feel safer because he does not want her to think that this means anything. It never does, he says, "It's all happening really to somebody else." He tells her that she is just another substitute for the laundromat. Marian then wonders if Duncan is also a substitute. He turns off the light but they are interrupted moments later by the arrival of his roommates.

Analysis

At the end of Part One, Marian goes over the events of the long weekend attempting to convince herself that she has made the right decision by agreeing to marry Peter. Part Two opens two months later and describes some of the changes that have occurred in Marian's life since her engagement. The most notable change, from a reader's perspective, is the shift in narrative voice: Marian's first-person narrative is now replaced by a third-person narration. Marian's ambivalent behaviour in the first part of the novel has already been discussed. It is thus interesting—and highly significant—that Marian should lose control of her story, of her own narrative, at the very moment when she gives *herself* to another person. By giving in to the pressures of what she thinks she ought to be doing, Marian, in this second part of the novel, drifts further and further away from what she described as her "true personality."

One of the things that is emphasized about Marian's present state of mind is the detachment from her immediate surroundings. Ever since her engagement, ever since she knew for sure that her position at the office was a temporary one, she has been uninterested in the events that go on there. She used to feel a sense of participation in the office turmoils but is now unable to involve herself. Instead, she continues to play the role that is expected of her by resolving to leave her job once she is married. Also notable is Marian's reason for sharing the news of her engagement with the three office virgins. She and Peter had decided to wait a while before making a public announcement but a general question relating to Peter catches her "desire to announce off-guard." Telling herself that the news will provide her colleagues with a glimmer of hope—if she could do it, they can too—Marian makes the announcement.

Marian is, at times, acutely aware of time. This is most evident when she receives the news that Clara has had her baby. After ending her conversation with Joe, Marian feels herself drifting towards a now not-so-very distant future. She feels helpless, as though she is moving with the "inevitability of water heading downhill," unable to influence events or her own destiny. Other people are making plans and arrangements while she lets the "current hold her up, trusting it to take her where she was going." She thinks of the days between now and her wedding as "landmark[s] to be passed on the shore"—days without any other purpose than "to measure the distance travelled." In the first section, Marian used similar words when running away from Peter, thinking of each post as "a distance-marker on [her] course." Now, instead of fleeing, Marian waits for the next phase of her life to begin.

As Marian waits, Duncan seeks distractions. Feeling tangled in his own words, caught on the treadmill of pointless and circular production, Duncan finds solace in the simple act of ironing. It is nice and easy and helps him combat his feeling that nothing ever gets done. He too feels detached from his surroundings and even tells Marian that he does not want her to think that their friendship means anything to him. "It's all happening really to somebody else," he tells her. She is simply a substitute for his restorative visits to the laundromat. Marian thinks that she too may be using Duncan as a substitute but does not know what it is he is supposed to be substituting. One possibility is that he allows Marian to forget, for the while that she is with him, the reality of the life that awaits her. When she first meets Duncan, she senses that in his presence, time seems to shift into slow-motion. Later in the novel, Marian explicitly states his association with the present moment: they had "no past and certainly no future." Experience and enjoyment of the present is something that is lacking in her relationship with Peter.

The significance of the girdle ad was discussed in the last section. Another good example of how expectations can be manipulated by the images and sounds around us is provided by the movie Marian sees. The film is a Western and portrays "bad people who were trying to do something evil and good people who were trying to stop them." The good people, Marian knows, would probably foil the bad people's plans by "getting to the money first." Knowing ahead of time what she is going to see, Marian does not bother to pay attention to the story: "Shortly there would be a sunset." What stands out in the information provided about this film is the predictability and repeatability of plots and narrative genres. Marian's lack of interest in the story and her ability to anticipate scenes reveal the long-lasting impact of repeated narratives and predictable formulas: her expectations of what will happen in this movie have been conditioned by what she has seen in countless other films. Similarly, readers of Atwood's novel will undoubtedly notice similarities in structure to many other novels and may already be trying to guess which of Marian's two suitors will, in the end, win her affection. These readers should perhaps ask themselves why they expect one particular ending over another, and what such an ending implies.

Study Questions

1. How has Marian's attitude towards her job changed since her engagement?

2. Why do Marian and her friends from work go to a fancy restaurant for lunch?

3. What are the three office virgins hoping to get from Marian following the announcement of her engagement?

4. What is the link between Peter and the "Underwear Man"?

5. What peculiar sensation overcomes Marian in the movie theatre?

6. Why has Marian been avoiding her friend Clara?

7. What does Marian think she has escaped when she leaves Clara's hospital room?

8. Explain Duncan's addiction to ironing.

9. What goes through Marian's mind as Duncan pulls her down beside him on his bed?

10. What is Duncan's reaction when he learns that Marian is engaged to be married?

Answers

1. Now that she is engaged, Marian knows that her job at Seymour Surveys is temporary. As a result, she views her surroundings with a certain amount of detachment and is unable to feel a sense of participation with the turmoil around her.

2. It is Lucy who suggests the fancier-than-usual restaurant. Lucy has been eating at fancier restaurants because she reasons that these are the places "the right kind of men might be expected to be lurking."

3. They want to know how Marian caught her man.

4. After hearing about the underwear man at work, Marian thinks that the mysterious, obscene caller might be Peter.

5. After realizing that the man from the laundromat is sitting next to her, Marian notices that her hand wanted to reach over and touch him on the shoulder.

6. She could not face another evening spent speculating on the mysterious behaviour of whatever was in Clara's belly. During the later stages of the pregnancy, Marian often forgot that Clara had any "perceptive faculties above the merely sentient and sponge-like."

7. During the visit, Marian is made to feel that the possibility of becoming a mother is now too close. She is also embarrassed by Clara's sentimental attitudes towards her husband. She describes Clara's life as the "mess she had blundered into." As she leaves, Marian feels glad that she is not Clara.

8. Duncan tells Marian that he is "not hooked" to ironing; he simply goes on binges. He thinks of it as a tension reducer, something to do with his hands. Duncan also explains that compared to the difficulty of putting together words, ironing is nice and simple and allows you to "straighten things out and get them flat."

9. Lying next to Duncan on his bed, Marian suspects that what he is really caressing is his own dressing gown and that she just happens to be in it.

10. It makes him feel safer. He wants Marian to know that this doesn't mean anything to him. It never does, he says, "It's all happening really to somebody else."

Suggested Essay Topics

1. Marian thinks of each day between now and her wedding as "a landmark to be passed on the shore." What is she waiting for? What does she expect will happen after she is married?

2. Duncan tells Marian that she is merely a substitute for his visits to the laundromat. What does he mean by this? A substitute for what? Discuss.

Chapters 17-19

Summary

Chapter 17 represents a turning point in the novel—and in Marian's life. Looking at Peter across a restaurant dinner table, Marian decides that anyone would have to agree that he is exceptionally handsome. Ainsley had once called him "nicely packaged" and Marian now thinks that she finds this quality attractive. She even feels a sense of "proud ownership" at being with him in this public place and reaches over to touch his hand. As they wait for their food to arrive, Marian and Peter resume a conversation begun earlier concerning the proper education of children. Peter talks theoretically but Marian believes that it is their own future children they are discussing. They disagree on a discipline issue and Peter accuses Marian of not understanding "these things." He tells her that she has led a sheltered life.

After a few moments, a dinner consisting of rare filet mignon wrapped in bacon is delivered to their table. As she eats, Marian's thoughts turn to the way Peter sometimes looks at her and touches

her in bed. She describes his touch as clinical and devoid of passion and likens the experience to that of a patient on a doctor's examination table. Her attention is then focused on Peter's plate. She watches him cut his meat and suddenly views the action as an act of violence. This thought triggers a series of others: she is reminded of the Moose Beer commercials for which she now feels responsible. This leads her to think of a newspaper story about a kid who shot nine people from an upstairs window—an example of removed violence. As she continues to watch Peter cut his food, she spontaneously visualizes the diagram of a planned cow, illustrating all the different cuts of meat. Looking down on her own plate, she no longer sees a steak but rather a hunk of muscle that was once "part of a real cow"—a cow that was whacked over the head "as it stood in a queue like someone waiting for a streetcar." She also thinks of the supermarket packaging that makes the meat appear official and clean. Unable to finish her dinner, Marian lays down her fork. At that same moment Peter smiles and says that "a good meal always makes you feel a little more human."

One day after the incident at the restaurant, Marian is unable to eat a pork chop and, a few weeks later, discovers that the planned pig and planned sheep, like the planned cow, are also "forbidden." She finds that she cannot eat anything with a bone, tendon, or fibre. She wonders what could possibly be making these decisions, deciding that it is certainly not her mind. She also begins to fear that the "refusal" will spread and thinks she might be becoming a vegetarian.

Meanwhile, Ainsley has learned that she is pregnant. She has told Len the news but has not informed him that she planned the pregnancy. As a result, Len, believing that he has impregnated "a little *girl*" becomes terribly upset and calls Marian for support. Marian guesses that Ainsley has not told Len the whole story and resents having to get involved. After all, it was not her concern since "she herself was getting married." When he shows up at her apartment a little while later, Marian offers him a beer (Moose Beer, bought "out of curiosity") and listens to him tell her how horrible he feels. Finally, Marian tells him that Ainsley intended to get pregnant. She tells him all about the anthropology courses that influenced Ainsley's thinking and how she is convinced that no woman can be fulfilled until she has had a child.

Len does not immediately believe Marian. Then, when he begins to understand what has happened, he makes a derogatory statement about the evils of educating women. Ainsley arrives soon afterwards and Len accuses her of using him. She tries to assure him that his work is done but he insists that he is already involved. An angry exchange ensues and Len breaks down, muttering something about his mother forcing him to eat an egg that he thought contained an unborn chick. Ainsley comforts him and Marian walks into the kitchen, revolted by the scene she has just witnessed. She thinks they are acting like infants and that Ainsley is already getting "a layer of blubber on her soul." She wonders, briefly, what she should do but decides that it is their problem and goes to her room. The next morning she discovers that she can no longer eat eggs.

The Christmas season arrives and with it the annual Seymour Surveys holiday office party. It is not an entirely festive event since many of the women resent the fact that they will have to return to work on the Friday following Christmas. Marian thinks of the Christmas parties of years past, heard about through some of the older girls, when the party had been a company-wide event. Now each department had its own little party. Sitting on a chesterfield with the three office virgins, Marian finds herself caught in the middle of a conversation between Lucy and Millie. Lucy is telling the story of a girl who lived with a friend of hers in London and who suddenly, and for no apparent reason, stopped washing. For two months the girl did not wash and wore the same clothes. Then, one day, she suddenly burned her clothes, took a bath, and has been normal ever since. Millie suggests that the girl was immature but Lucy thinks she was sick. Marian's mind focuses on the word immature: "you were green and then you ripened, became mature." She associates this with dresses for the mature figure and, looking around the room, notices that all of the women are eating. Each one is wearing a dress for the mature figure. She then imagines that they are all attached to an invisible vine by a stem at the tops of their heads, hanging in various stages of decay. She considers that she will one day be like them, then realizes that she already is one of them. Suffocated by the "sargasso-sea of femininity," Marian feels the desire for something solid and clear: a man, Peter.

At that very moment, Mrs. Bogue decides to announce the news of Marian's engagement. Having heard that Mrs. Bogue preferred her girls to be either unmarried or seasoned veterans with their "liability to unpredictable pregnancies" well behind them, Marian figures that she will now be expected to leave her job. Marian leaves the party soon afterwards, takes the subway, and goes for a walk. As she walks, she thinks of tomorrow's trip to visit her parents and how they and other relatives no longer seem to belong to her. She then thinks of Peter and of the present she had finally decided to get him: a book on cameras. As she walks through a park near the university, she feels jealous of the buildings that were once hers: she would have liked them to vanish, yet there they remained, as unconcerned about her absence as they had been about her presence. She stops to listen to the distant sounds of the city, thinking: "You have to watch it, you don't want to end up not taking baths."

At the party, Marian had felt herself "close to some edge" but now those reactions seemed silly. She decides that there are simply certain things that she has to get through between now and the wedding and that afterwards "it would be all right." Just as she decides that she is almost ready to go home, wrap her presents, and eat half a cow, she hears a voice. It is Duncan sitting on a snowy park bench. She sits down beside him, undoes the buttons of his overcoat and huddles herself inside it. She strokes his shaggy sweater and feels his spare body underneath. They sit without moving and, for a moment, time outside the park vanishes. She feels herself becoming numb and notices that her feet no longer ache. Finally Duncan says: "You took a long time, I've been expecting you." Marian, beginning to shiver, responds simply: "I have to go now."

Analysis

Sitting in a restaurant at the beginning of Chapter 17, Marian reveals an ever-increasing identification with the commercially conventional as she contemplates Peter's superficial qualities. She admires Peter's good looks and decides that being "nicely packaged" is a good quality to have. She also finds comfort in the idea of consensus: her belief that Peter would be considered good looking by everybody provides her with a sense of "proud ownership." The fact that Marian derives pleasure from Peter's presumed universal attractiveness reveals her own attraction to what is safe and standardized. Also admired is Peter's ability to make decisions. When the time comes to order their dinners, Marian, staring down at the menu, feels only "vacillation." Peter, on the other hand, is able to "make up their minds right away." Of course, the bigger problem is that Marian does not think to consider choices not offered on any menu. A menu suggests limited, predetermined options; it provides one with an illusion of choice. Marian feels trapped by the options presented to her at work and by her personal life yet does not consider the possibility of straying from the seemingly unavoidable possibilities. Could it be because she, like everyone else around her, has been conditioned to accept those options without questioning them? Conditioned not to resist and to believe that there are no other options available?

Marian's indecision is followed by thoughts of intimate moments shared with Peter. We learn that Peter's bedroom gaze and touch (described as passionless and clinical) evoke in Marian thoughts of a patient on an examination table. She also wonders if Peter has purchased a marriage manual—an act that would be consistent with his personality. This, of course, suggests a lack of imagination and an unwillingness to stray from accepted and usual ways of doing things. It also demonstrates a readiness to believe and trust, a misguided faith in the advice dished out in mass-market self-help guides. Because such guides are displayed in respectable bookstores and come packaged in official looking shells, they are purchased under the assumption that the author must be an authority. That Peter is the kind of person likely to buy one of these guides (according to Marian) may account for the roles he thinks Marian and he should assume.

Marian's thoughts, stirred by the sight of Peter cutting his meat, now turn to violence. This subject leads her to consider the ads for Moose Beer that are now appearing "everywhere." Marian would like to believe that the ads are not doing any harm but cannot help feeling "partially responsible" for them. Reflecting on the content of the ad, Marian notes how "unreal" it is and how the image it represents does not reflect a true reality. It is "too tidy" and "posed" —it creates the illusion of something that does not actually exist. *Remember that in Chapter 3, the ad is said to depict a typical "sportsman" and is designed to appeal to the average beer-drinker.* Because it is seen by everyone in the city, thus becoming a common reference for many people, it takes on a reality that it does not inherently possess. Such is the power of the media image. *Remember, too, Marian's conclusions about the girdle ad.*

The repercussions of this image bombardment are expressed in Marian's next thought. Marian remembers reading about a young boy who shot nine people from an upstairs window. The shooter's position, a safe distance from his targets below, informs us (as does the narrative itself) that this is an example of "removed violence." Marian remembers how the boy looked like someone who would never even throw a punch but, because of his detached and seemingly safe position, is able to do things he would not do otherwise: "the finger guiding but never touching." The actions of the lone shooter are not dissimilar to the strategies and campaigns used in the world of advertising: like a person shooting from a rooftop, advertising images attack countless and unseen numbers of people by invading their mental space and assaulting their world view. Perhaps this accounts for Marian's feelings of responsibility concerning the beer campaign.

Marian's thoughts eventually lead her to imagine the diagram of a planned cow. She compares the visual image of a cow being knocked over the head and killed to the nicely packaged, labelled, and priced products offered on supermarket shelves. It is here that Marian's body begins its "protest" by refusing to eat anything that was once alive. While Marian remains, for quite some time, unaware of the reasons for her body's peculiar actions, critics have offered many different explanations for the eating disorder. One interesting interpretation proposes that Marian displays the symptoms of anorexia nervosa. Elspeth Cameron (1985), for example, claims that recent medical information offers a "useful key" for interpreting the text. Cameron acknowledges that Atwood knew nothing of the disease when she wrote the novel but argues that Marian displays almost all of the main symptoms of the eating disorder: a feeling of ineffectiveness, a fear of fat, and the longing for autonomy. The structure of the novel, Cameron claims, is even based on the three stages of the illness: Part One shows the "background causes," Part Two "the mind/body split that accompanies the onset of actual diet restriction," and Part Three dramatizes "the spontaneous resolution of the illness." Cameron's reading is certainly interesting and useful, but readers should be wary of critics bearing magic keys that seemingly unlock all of a text's hidden secrets. No such key exists, nor does a definitive reading of this or any other text.

After an unenjoyable evening at her office Christmas party, Marian reaches a point where she feels just about ready to move ahead. She tells herself that she will soon make it through this period of waiting and that everything will then be all right. She convinces herself that the fears she was experiencing earlier in the evening—feeling "dangerously close to some edge"—were "rather silly." In other words, Marian here does to herself what she has been letting others do for quite some time: she manipulates her thoughts in order to disregard her true feelings. She plans to go home and prepare for her trip to visit her parents. She even feels hungry enough to "devour half a cow, dotted lines and all." But just as she is about to act on these decisions, a voice calls out from the snowy trees behind her. It is, of course, Duncan's voice. Without speaking, Marian joins Duncan on the bench, huddles herself inside his overcoat, and shelters herself from the world around her. In his presence, in this present moment, "time outside the white circle of the Park [vanishes]" and her future with Peter is briefly forgotten.

Study Questions

1. Describe Marian's feelings towards Peter as they sit together in the restaurant.

2. What triggers Marian's thought of the diagram of the planned cow?

3. What does Marian make of her inability to eat certain foods?

4. Does Peter have any difficulty finishing his steak? What does he say when he is finished eating?

5. What brand of beer does Marian offer Len? Why did she choose to buy this particular brand?

6. After learning that Ainsley planned to get pregnant, Len makes a comment concerning women and college education. What does he say?

7. At the office Christmas party, Marian sits with Lucy, Millie, and Emmy even though they are now treating her coolly. Why has their behaviour towards Marian changed?

8. What does Marian buy Peter for Christmas?

9. Is there any evidence in the text that Marian is somehow affected by the story about the girl who stopped washing?

10. Walking in the snowy park near the university, Marian decides that she is just about ready to go home and eat half a cow. What stops her?

Answers

1. Marian thinks of Peter as "nicely packaged" and, sitting with him here in this public place, feels a sense of "proud ownership."

2. Watching Peter cut his meat leads to thoughts about Moose Beer commercials, removed violence, and the cow diagram.

3. Marian is certain that it is not her mind making the decisions to reject certain foods. She is afraid that the refusal will spread and that she might become a vegetarian.

4. As Peter cleans off his plate, he says: "A good meal always

makes you feel a little more human."

5.   Marian offers Len Moose Beer. She bought it "out of curiosity" but discovers that it tastes just like any other brand.

6.   "That's what we get then for educating women. They get all kinds of ridiculous ideas."

7.   They know that Marian is on the "fringe of matrimony" and thus no longer genuinely single and no longer able to empathize with their problems.

8.   Marian buys Peter a technical book about cameras.

9.   Walking home after the party, Marian tells herself that she will have to be careful, "you don't want to end up not taking baths."

10.   Marian is stopped by the sound of Duncan's voice.

Suggested Essay Topics

1.   Marian thinks of Peter as "nicely packaged." Discuss Marian's feelings for her future husband.

2.   Should Marian feel responsible for the Moose Beer ads? Why? Why not?

3.   Duncan, sitting on a park bench, unexpectedly calls out to Marian at a very crucial moment. Discuss the significance of this scene.

Chapters 20-22

Summary

Chapter 20 opens with a description of Marian "walking slowly down the aisle" to the sound of gentle music. It is not until she reads one of the items on her grocery list that the aisle in question becomes identifiable as the aisle of a supermarket and not a church. She notices the inescapable music and, knowing that it is deliberately used to lull shoppers into a "euphoric trance" and lower sales resistance, feels resentment towards it. But knowing about these

kinds of sales strategies does not make Marian immune to them. Recently, she has found herself pushing shopping carts "like a somnambulist" and, as a result, now tries to defend herself by making lists. However, she knows that this precaution will be only partially successful. Her position at Seymour Surveys has taught her that products are all essentially the same. The only way you can make a choice, she thinks, is to abandon yourself to the music and make a random snatch. Eventually, she will have to make a choice, thereby validating what some planner or marketing strategist had hoped and predicted she would do.

Picking through the vegetables, Marian wishes that she could once again become a carnivore. She recalls her trip back home at Christmas: at dinner she had said that she was not hungry and then, secretly, had eaten huge quantities of cranberry sauce, mashed potatoes, and mince pie. She thinks, too, of her family's reaction to her engagement—a rather smug satisfaction, as though their fears about the repercussions of a university education had finally been calmed. Now that she was engaged, they figured she was turning out right after all (even though they had not yet met Peter).

Now an officially engaged couple, Marian and Peter see more of each other. In fact, ever since Marian was "ringed," Peter has developed a habit of "displaying her" to his well-dressed and soon-to-be successful friends. Deciding that the time has come for Peter to get to know some of her friends, Marian makes plans for a dinner party with Clara and Joe but then worries about the menu. Over the past month, the last forms of meat that she had been able to eat—hamburger, pork, lamb, and hot dogs—had excluded themselves from her diet. She decides on a casserole.

By the night of the dinner, Marian has become quite annoyed by her body's decision to reject certain foods. Because she is now unable to eat anything that was once alive, she thinks that her stand might be an ethical one. However, immediately following this realization she discovers that she can no longer eat carrots. She manages to get through dinner without incident but the evening is not a success. Clara and Joe had been unable to find a babysitter and had thus brought their children with them. All three are eventually pacified and put to sleep but the ensuing conversation is awkward. After their guests leave Peter tells Marian, jokingly, that they will "never be like that." Marian then tries to convince herself that it does not matter whether or not Peter gets along with Clara and Joe because they were from her past. Peter, she thinks, should not be expected to adjust to her past: it was the future that mattered.

Later that night, Ainsley returns home from her Pre-Natal Clinic. On the verge of tears, she tells Marian about a psychologist who this evening spoke about the importance of the father image for a child. Without one, Ainsley reports, a boy is "absolutely *certain* to turn into a. . . homosexual." The mention of this "one category of man who had never shown the slightest interest in her" fills her eyes with tears. She then sits up, pushes back her hair and exclaims: "There's got to be a way."

In the next chapter, Marian and Duncan enter a downtown museum holding hands. They have been seeing a lot of each other lately, by collusion now rather than coincidence. Duncan is now writing a new term paper and has been stuck on the opening sentence for two and a half weeks. As a result, he feels the need for frequent escapes. On this particular day, he phoned Marian to tell her that he craved the museum and, since Peter would never go there, she agreed to join him. Even though she thinks that her friendship with Duncan has nothing to do with Peter, Marian dreads an encounter between the two men. She fears that such a meeting would lead to the destruction of one of the two by the other.

As they walk through the museum, we learn that Marian once asked Duncan why he does not find himself a female graduate student. His answer was that such a person would not be an escape. Marian figures that she is being used by Duncan but decides that she does not mind as long as she knows what she is being used for. In fact, she finds Duncan's complete self-centredness reassuring and is not disturbed when he tells her that he does not even like her very much. It does not disturb her because she does not have to answer. Conversely, when Peter tells her that he loves her, she feels the need to exert herself. She guesses that she too is using Duncan but cannot figure out her motives. She then thinks of the life she has led over the past few months, characterizing it as "a period of waiting": she was merely drifting with the current, waiting for an event in the future determined by an event in the past. However, with Duncan she was caught in the present—they had "no past and certainly no future."

Duncan leads Marian into the Ancient Egyptian section of the museum to show her his favourite mummy cases. As they browse through the death-filled room, Duncan tells Marian that he sometimes thinks he would like to live forever. He shares his thoughts on mutability and tells her of his desire to stop time. He then shows her his "womb-symbol"—a skeleton, still partly covered with skin, lying on its side with its legs drawn up. Duncan explains that it is pre-pyramid, preserved by the sands of the desert and tells her that when he gets "really fed up with this place" he's going to go dig himself in somewhere. Marian is contemplating the stunted figure, feeling somewhat sorry for it, when she notices that Duncan is reaching out to touch her. He bends to kiss her but she swerves and rests her head on his shoulder. A passing guard approaches to tell them that kissing in the Mummy Room is not permitted.

Sitting in the museum coffee shop a little while later, Duncan casually suggests that it might be a good idea if they went to bed together. Marian, who has been justifying her relationship with Duncan on the grounds that it was innocent, rejects the idea and reminds him that she will soon be married (in a month). Duncan views this as her problem—he thought it was a good idea for himself. He tells her that he does not find her particularly desirable but thought that she would at least know how and would be sensible about it. He also thinks that it would be a good idea for him to get over this thing he has about sex. What he means, he explains, is he suspects he may be a latent homosexual, or a latent heterosexual—either way, he says, he's pretty latent. He tells Marian that although he's taken several stabs at it, he always begins to think about the futility of it all and gives up. Whenever he's writing term papers he thinks about sex and then, when he's got a "willing lovely. . . all set up for the *coup de grace*," he can think only of term papers. It's an alternation of distractions, he says. Marian thinks she should be insulted by the impersonality of his request, but is not. Instead, she feels as though she should do something helpful so she takes Duncan's pulse.

Duncan's roommates happen to be sitting at another table in the coffee shop and invite Marian back to their apartment for dinner. Marian accepts but then remembers her eating problem. She explains to Duncan that she has not been eating certain foods lately and that it might be better if she does not go. Duncan, however, assures her that they will work something out. Marian apologizes and, after explaining that she cannot account for her eating problems, Duncan suggests that her behaviour is probably "representative of modern youth." He tells her that she is "rebelling against the system."

When they arrive at Duncan's apartment, Marian, hoping to prevent unnecessary complications with the roommates who do not know that she is engaged and who probably assume she and Duncan are involved, removes her engagement ring. They are greeted at the door by an apronned Trevor who immediately runs off to attend to his kitchen. Inside, Fish sits locked into his chair by a board resting across the arms and is busily writing. Marian asks him about his work and unwittingly initiates a long and detailed account of his latest theories on Lewis Carroll's *Alice's Adventures in Wonderland*. He explains that *Alice* is a sexual-identity-crisis book about a little girl trying to find her role as a woman. One sexual role after another emerges but she is unable to accept any of them. (There is also an obsession with time.) According to his theory, Alice makes many attempts but, by the end of the book, has not really reached anything that could be called maturity. Duncan snickers at Fish's interpretation and Trevor remarks that he does not approve of his roommate's drunken "Viennese" criticism.

Trevor announces that dinner is ready and the foursome sit at the makeshift dining table consisting of two card tables pushed close together. Marian now begins to worry about how she will dispose of the uneatables on her plate. Trevor makes a timely comment about how important eating is ("why eat just to stay alive as most people do?") and talks of his sauce—his own, not the standardized store-bought bottled variety. Fish continues to talk about his proposed thesis topic, a complicated argument incorporating birthrates, poetry, and statistics, and Marian becomes entranced by his ability to eat and talk simultaneously. As the dinner progresses, Marian becomes caught between Trevor's and Fish's simultaneous dialogues—Trevor going on about his dinner and Fish still expounding on his thesis. The scene becomes almost chaotic: Trevor runs in and out of the kitchen, bringing and removing various dishes and then suddenly appears with a flaming skewer in each hand. When he slides "whatever was impaled on the skewers" onto Marian's plate, she realizes that most of her meal is meat. She knocks Duncan on the shin to get his attention and proceeds to fling the chunks of meat to him across the table. Oblivious to the airborne food, Fish stands up and accidentally jackknifes the table legs. His plate falls onto his lap and a just-tossed piece of meat hits Duncan on the side of his head. Trevor arrives from the kitchen just in time to watch the scene unfold.

After dinner Duncan walks Marian part of the way home. A reference to Duncan's home life prompts Marian to suggest that he might want to consider moving out. He dismisses this idea saying that his roommates take good care of him and spend much time fussing about his identity. Duncan believes that his roommates see themselves as his surrogate parents and is content with their concern for him. He then reintroduces his idea of going to bed together. This time, Marian entertains the idea for a few moments but they are unable to figure out the logistics and the topic is once again dropped. They sit near a baseball park and Marian admires the blank space of untracked snow. Suddenly, she is filled with the desire to run and jump in it, to make footmarks and "irregular paths." She knows, however, that she will soon be walking, sedately as ever, across the snow towards the station. She stands up and asks Duncan if he is coming any further. He says no and walks away. Marian retrieves her engagement ring from her change purse and walks to the subway station.

Analysis

In previous chapters, Marian has contemplated Peter's more superficial qualities and has even gone so far as to think of him as an object belonging to her. Here, walking down the aisle of a supermarket, the commercial nature of their quickly approaching marital/material partnership is made explicit. The first few lines of Chapter 20 lead the reader to believe that the aisle in question is that of a church and that we have now skipped ahead to the day of

Marian and Peter's wedding. When it turns out to be the aisle of a supermarket, the lingering aftereffect of our own erroneous presumption reminds us of just how similar the two "aisle" scenes can actually be.

Also of significance in this scene at the supermarket is the music. Marian knows that it is filtered into the store in order to lull shoppers into a trance-like state which lowers sales resistance. Yet, she is not immune to it. The description of how and why the music is used provides another revealing look at the strategies employed by the corporate advertising machine. Also, the fact that Marian is aware of these strategies provides a better understanding of the guilt she feels over the Moose Beer ads. Nevertheless, Marian feels that the only way to make a choice between products that are all essentially the same is to "abandon yourself to the soothing music and make a random snatch." In other words, she accepts being the victim of these commercial manipulations and, once again, accepts the choices that are offered to her. By doing so, she again does what is expected of her—this time by some corporate planner.

The reaction of Marian's family to the news that she is getting married is also worth examining. Above all, they are satisfied and relieved that Marian's university education has not led her astray. By getting engaged, Marian wins the approval of her parents by proving, in their minds, that she is turning out all right. The supposed dangers of a university education in the lives of women is a subject that comes up throughout the novel. For example, Len blames Ainsley's university education for giving her the "ridiculous idea" that her femininity will only be fulfilled once she has a baby. Similarly, in Chapter 27, Joe explains to Marian that life is harder for women who have been to university because they grow accustomed to being treated "like a thinking human being." He goes so far as to suggest that it may be better if women were not "allowed to go to university at all." In short, education is seen as a threat to a woman's feminine passivity. Marian gains the approval of her parents by showing that she is still willing to comply. Peter's approval is manifested in the pride he takes in introducing his new fiancée to his "more official" friends: now that Marian is ringed she, like the jewel on her finger, becomes an object worthy of display.

After a disappointing evening with Clara and Joe, Marian decides that it does not matter whether or not Peter likes her old friends since they were from her past. She believes that, in her relationship with Peter, "it was the future that mattered"—a belief that is consistent with Marian's passive waiting. What Marian neglects to consider, however, is the present. When thinking of Peter, Marian tends to look ahead to the distant future. She likes to think of Peter's hobbies, for example, because she believes that they will make him less likely to have a heart attack when he gets older. But rarely does Marian think positively about her present situation with her fiancé. In fact, she characterizes the recent past (the period of her engagement to Peter) as an "endurance of time marked by no real event." With Duncan, however, Marian feels caught in an "eddy of present time" (examples of this have been discussed in previous sections). She notes that he does not appear to care what happens to her after she passes out of the "range of his perpetual present" but finds this "lack of interest" comforting—perhaps because he is not trying to change or control her.

In a previous section of these notes, an interpretation was offered (Cameron, 1985) suggesting that Marian's eating problems might be symptomatic of a true eating disorder, anorexia nervosa. Duncan proposes another diagnosis. According to him, Marian's eating problems are "representative of modern youth"; she is, in his words, "rebelling against the system." He does not state what it is he thinks that Marian's body is rebelling against, but if one relates digestion to consumption, it is possible to think of the protest in the following terms: by restricting the intake of food, Marian's body is, in effect, protesting against the fact that Marian consumes all that is fed to her, willingly assimilating and internalizing the ideas, expectations, and beliefs of the world around her. These ideas, expectations, and beliefs then become part of her (for example, Marian's decision to quit her job, the flannelly voice that abdicates decision-making responsibilities. . .) and contribute to her own exploitation by eating away at her beliefs and sense of identity. Such an internal division also helps explain the shift from a first- to a third-person narrative.

Duncan is not the only character in this section who tries to influence the reader's interpretation of the novel. Fish offers a diagnosis of his own by providing readers with an analysis of Lewis Carroll's *Alice's Adventures in Wonderland* that sounds just as plausible in relation to Marian as it does to Alice. According to Fish, *Alice* is a "sexual-identity-crisis-book" about a young girl trying to find her role as a woman. Many different sexual roles are presented to Alice but she is unable to accept any of them. He adds that Alice makes many attempts but "refuses to commit herself." In the end, Fish says, you can't say that "she has reached anything that can be definitely called maturity." At this point in the novel, it remains to be seen whether or not Marian will reach something akin to maturity, but the apparent parallels between Alice and Marian are striking just the same. David Harkness (1989) has examined these parallels in much detail and argues that Atwood's use of Carroll's story is not restricted to these instances. In fact, Harkness suggests that there are strong "intertextual links" to both *Alice's Adventures in Wonderland* and to the second book, *Through the Looking Glass and What Alice Found There*, that can enrich our understanding of the novel's structure and Marian's eating disorder. Of course, the parallels between the two (or three) texts should not be thought of as evidence for a definitive reading of Atwood's novel. Similarly, excessive credulity in the interpretation expressed by Fish could limit one's understanding of other complexities found within the novel. Given the difficulties experienced by Marian as she struggles to find her identity in a male-dominated business world, it is perhaps wise to view this attempt to define Marian's condition with suspicion.

At the end of this section, Marian and Duncan sit on the snow-covered ground near a baseball park. As she looks at the fresh, untracked snow that surrounds her, Marian suddenly longs to "run and jump in it." She wants to run where suggested paths and directions have not yet been mapped or charted, where there are no restrictions or guiding signs. She wants to make "irregular paths." In other words, Marian appears to be looking away from the menu of suggested options (see Analysis, Section 5). She knows, however, that she will soon be walking "sedately as ever. . . towards the station." And, sure enough, when Marian begins to make her way towards the station, the imagined frolic in the snow is not realized. Instead, she retrieves her engagement ring from her change purse.

Study Questions

1. Why does Marian resent the music that is filtered through the aisles of the supermarket?

2. How does Marian's knowledge of marketing strategies help protect her against the various schemes used to increase the desire to buy?

3. Earlier in the novel, Len made a comment about women and education. In Chapter 20, a similar view is expressed. What is it?

4. Marian's dinner party is not a success. After her guests have left, Peter decides that he and Marian will never be like Clara and Joe. Marian decides that it does not matter if Peter does not get along with them—why?

5. According to Duncan, what do sex and the writing of term papers have in common?

6. After being invited to dinner by Duncan's roommate, Trevor, Marian tells Duncan about her eating problem. What is his diagnosis?

7. Summarize Fish's reading of *Alice's Adventures in Wonderland.*

8. Walking home after dinner, Marian asks Duncan why he does not consider moving. What is his answer?

9. When Marian and Duncan stop to sit near a baseball park, what does Marian suddenly get the urge to do?

10. Before dinner, Marian removed her engagement ring. Where did she put it?

Answers

1. Because she knows why it is there: it is supposed to lull shoppers into a "euphoric trance" and lower sales resistance to the point where "all things are desirable."

2. Knowing what "they were up to" does not make Marian immune. She knows that there are no real differences among the various brands of the same product but still finds her-

self pushing shopping carts "like a somnambulist" and "twitching with the impulse" to buy.

3. Marian recalls her family's reaction to the news of her engagement: they were smugly satisfied, "as though their fears about the effects of her university education. . . had been calmed at last."

4. Marian decides that it does not matter because Clara and Joe were from her past. Peter belongs to her future.

5. Both are distractions.

6. Duncan thinks that Marian is probably "representative of modern youth" and that she is "rebelling against the system."

7. Fish argues that *Alice* is a book about a little girl trying to find her role as a woman. Various sexual roles are presented to her but she is unable to accept any of them. By the end of the book, Alice has not achieved a definite maturity.

8. Duncan tells Marian that his roommates take good care of him and spend much time fussing about his identity.

9. Marian notices the powdery, untracked snow and suddenly wants to get up and run through it. She wants to make "irregular paths."

10. She puts it in her change purse.

Suggested Essay Topics

1. Marian knows why there is music playing at the supermarket. However, her awareness does not make her immune to its effects. Should it? Explain.

2. Why is Marian's family so pleased to hear the news of her engagement to Peter?

Chapters 23-25

Summary

It is the day after Valentine's Day and Marian and Peter are lying together in bed. As Peter enjoys a scotch and a cigarette, dumping his ashes in an ashtray placed on his fiancée's bare back, Marian worries. Earlier that day her body finally rejected rice pudding, something that had been acceptable for weeks. She has tried, ever since her eating problem began, to pretend that there is nothing really wrong with her. She thought and hoped that the problem would eventually go away on its own. Now forced to confront the problem, Marian questions her own normality and fears Peter will think her a freak and postpone the wedding.

Earlier in the day, Marian had felt the need to discuss her feelings and paid an after-work visit to Clara. But instead of the comfort she had hoped to receive from her friend, the visit makes her feel envious. Marian finds Clara sitting in a playpen with her second youngest and realizes that "whatever was going to happen to [her] had already happened." Clara had already become what she was going to be. Although Marian would not want to trade places with Clara, she would like to know what she is becoming. The thought of waking up one day and discovering that she has already changed fills her with dread. She wants to know what direction her life is taking so that she can be prepared. She finally tells Clara about her eating problem and asks if she thinks that she is normal. Clara assures Marian that she is "almost abnormally normal" and that she is probably just suffering from bridal nerves.

However, lying in bed with Peter, Marian is still not convinced. She asks Peter the same question she asked Clara and he tells her that she is "marvellously normal." He then asks her to get him a drink and flip the record. Marian goes to the kitchen and cuts two pieces of the Valentine's Day cake she bought for Peter. She takes a bite but is unable to eat it. She decides to give the cake to Peter as a sort of test: if he could not eat it either then she would know that she is normal. They make love and, afterwards, Peter eats the cake while Marian lies on her stomach with the ashtray on her back.

Following Peter's request, Marian spends an afternoon at the

hairdresser readying herself for a party he is hosting. Peter also hinted that Marian should buy a new dress and, dutifully, she chooses a red sequined thing that she does not really like. She is not very fond of her new coif either. Every strand of hair is glued in place and styled in a fashion to which she is not accustomed. The hairdresser's treatment of her head leads her to compare it to a cake: it is "something to be carefully iced and ornamented." She likens the passivity of the beautification process to that of a patient being admitted into a hospital for an operation. She feels as though she should be anaesthetized while all the necessary details are taken care of.

When all of the curlers and pins are properly fastened, Marian is led to an assembly line of hair dryers where rows of identical women sit under identical machines. She feels totally inert and wonders if this is what she is being pushed towards: a "compound of the simply vegetable and the simply mechanical." She then resigns herself to the "necessity of endurance" and picks up a movie star magazine. The caption on the back reads: "Girls! Be Successful! If You Want to Really Go Places, Develop Your Bust. . . "

Finally, Marian gets to see the finished product and realizes that they have manufactured something completely artificial looking. To her, the excessive styling makes her look like a call girl. The hairdresser, however, tells her that she should wear her hair like this more often. She considers asking him to comb out some of the effects but is intimidated by the official surroundings and figures he must know what is right. Because she had "walked through that. . . door of her own free will" she decides that she had better accept the consequences. She then thinks that Peter will probably like it.

On her way to the subway, Marian walks through a large department store and finds herself in the household wares department. She is reminded of the shower the girls at the office gave her the day before (her last day of work) and of the anxious letters she has been receiving from home urging her to hurry and choose her patterns. A cluster of women with shopping bags stand watching a man demonstrate a grater and Marian hovers, briefly, on the fringes to take a look. She soon loses interest and returns home.

Marian arrives at the apartment just as Ainsley and Len are

having a heated argument. Marian tries to avoid getting involved but is coerced into the room by Ainsley. Still convinced that a boy raised without a father will be a homosexual, Ainsley now wants Len to marry her. Len, on other hand, wants Ainsley to have an abortion and claims that it was all her doing. They argue about who seduced who and about whose responsibility it is and Marian finally tells them to be quiet in case the landlady hears them. Len, by now very upset, yells "SCREW the lady down below!" Marian and Ainsley both laugh at this remark and Len gets even angrier. He tells Ainsley to go to hell and stomps down the stairs, attracting the attention of the landlady and her guests who were quietly enjoying afternoon tea. Ainsley runs after him, and Marian, driven not by the sense that she could do something but by "some obscure herd- or lemming-instinct," follows. When he reaches the bottom of the first flight of stairs Len shouts: "You'll never get me." He then continues his descent and bursts out the door. Back upstairs Ainsley tells Marian that she will simply have to find another man to provide her baby with a father image. Marian, thinking that there is nothing she could do anyway, decides that she does not want to know what Ainsley's plan is and considers the matter settled.

Later in the day, but still too early to get dressed, Marian wanders through her apartment looking for something to do to pass the time. Remembering that she has not yet eaten, she goes into the kitchen and opens the fridge. It is filled with items that have been there longer than she cares to remember. The counter and sink, filled with scummy unwashed dishes, is worse. She gets a sudden urge to clean the entire mess but decides to leave it, thinking that the mould may have as much right to life as she has. Instead she goes downstairs to take a bath. As she removes her engagement ring she is reminded of the fact that it is a bit too large for her. Peter had wanted to have it cut down to size but Clara told Marian not to since fingers tend to swell with age and pregnancies. Marian has developed a fear of seeing the ring disappear down the drain.

As she lies in the tub, Marian notices a reflection in the two taps and spout. It takes her a moment to recognize that the bulging and distorted forms are her own body. She then notices that the water is covered with a film of soap and dirt, and fears that she is dissolving. She gets out of the tub and puts on her ring, considering it for a moment as a "protective talisman" that would keep her together.

When she gets upstairs, Marian, still in a state of panic, decides that she cannot face Peter's party. She does not really know Peter's friends and is afraid that she may lose her shape. As she contemplates the red dress hanging in her closet, she wonders what she can possibly do. A "formless unhappiness" overwhelms her, a feeling that seems to have been with her for some time. Her attention is drawn to the two dolls on top of her dresser. Placed on either side of the mirror, the dolls appear to be watching her. Marian looks at herself in the mirror and gets the impression that she is inside the dolls looking down at herself on the bed. Each doll sees something slightly different: the blonde one notices Marian's hair and nails whereas the dark one looks deeper "at something she could not quite see." The two images are described as drawing further and further away from each other while the centre "that held them together, would soon be quite empty." Marian thinks that the dolls' separate visions are trying to pull her apart.

Marian suddenly gets up and calls Duncan. She tells him that she needs him to come to the party. Duncan agrees and the relief Marian feels prompts her to invite Clara, Joe, Ainsley, and the office virgins. This, she thinks, is the answer: to ensure that there are people at the party who really know her. Now strengthened by the knowledge that her friends will be there, Marian begins to dress. She puts on the girdle she bought to go with the red dress and asks Ainsley to do up her zipper. Ainsley likes the dress and lends Marian a pair of gold chunky earrings to go with it. She also does Marian's makeup. When she is done, Marian looks in the mirror and sees the eyes of a person she does not recognize.

While Marian is practicing how to move her new face, the landlady comes up to inform Ainsley that she will have to move out. The landlady tells Ainsley that although she put up with the drinking, untidiness, and overnight gentlemen visitors, now that her drunken and disreputable friends have been brought out into the open, she would have to go. In response, Ainsley accuses the woman of being a hypocrite who is merely worried about what the neighbours will say. She informs the landlady that she is going to have a baby and would not want to bring "him" up in a house where she would teach him dishonesty. She then accuses the landlady of being the most "anti-Creative Life Force" she has ever met and assures her that she is only too happy to leave. Outraged, the landlady turns pale and descends the stairs emitting cries of dismay. Marian feels safely removed from these complications and wonders why she had ever been afraid of the lady below—she was so easily deflated. Shortly afterwards, Peter arrives and he and Marian leave to prepare for the party.

Analysis

Beginning and ending with the image of Marian lying in bed, an ashtray on her back and Peter at her side, Chapter 23 provides a glimpse into the couple's private life together. On this night, Peter enjoys a scotch and cigarette while Marian worries. Until now, she has tried to convince herself that there is nothing actually wrong with her and that her eating problem will eventually go away on its own. But Marian realizes that the problem is not getting better, in fact, it is becoming worse. She is plagued by thoughts that she may not be normal and is reluctant to speak frankly to her future husband for fear he will think her neurotic and postpone the wedding. Ainsley tries to convince her that "nobody is normal" but Marian continues to worry. Clara's words are more reassuring; she tells Marian that she is "almost abnormally normal" and that she will eventually "get over" her eating problem. Fittingly, this is the exact same thing Marian was told when she expressed concern over her company's mandatory pension plan. Clara's words of consolation do not imply that Marian's problem will get better, only that she will grow accustomed to whatever it is that is causing it. In other words, she will learn to adjust. Marian's problem, and the factors causing it, are left unexamined and unchallenged.

Marian's worries are momentarily interrupted when she notices the miniature aircraft carrier on Peter's desk. The carrier is the product of Peter's new hobby: "putting together model ships from model ship kits." Marian gets involved by reading out the instructions and handing Peter the pieces. The passing reference to this activity is significant because it is one of the only activities

Marian and Peter do together. Unsurprisingly, it shows the couple engaged in a project requiring hardly any imagination or creativity; even their recreation is done by the book. Equally revealing about their relationship is the cake Marian gives Peter for Valentine's Day. Marian does not buy the cake to show her love for Peter; she buys it out of guilt. Pink, heart-shaped, and "probably stale," the cake is a "token" representative of their relationship—a gift so clichéd and uninspired that it is almost meaningless. Any sentiments conveyed through this cake can be no less artificial than the coloured icing masking the bland staleness within. Marian appears to realize this and is unable to eat even a single bite. In fact, she spits it out, thereby spitting out her own artificial and insincere display of affection. Of course, the fact that Marian presents Peter with a cake is notable for another reason: it foreshadows the cake offered to Peter in the final pages of the novel. Interestingly, both cakes are intended to act as a kind of test but it is Peter's performance on the second of these examinations that proves more meaningful.

When the day of Peter's party arrives, Marian complies with her future hubby's requests to buy a new dress and get her hair done. Persuaded by a saleslady's flattery, Marian chooses a dress that she does not really like and then, at the hairdresser's, allows herself to be made into something she can barely recognize. She finds the whole experience at the salon an exercise in passivity, comparing the procedure to an operation and concluding that she may as well be anaesthetized while all of the "necessary physical details" are taken care of. She dislikes the feeling of being treated like an object but fails to realize that the treatment she is undergoing in this factory of sameness is merely a slight exaggeration of the standardization she allows herself to go through every day.

Installed under a hair dryer, Marian finds herself part of an assembly line of identical women, all waiting patiently while the beautification domes do their magic work. Marian wonders if this "inert" and "simply vegetable" existence is what she is being pushed towards but carries on with the procedure just the same. She eventually resigns herself to the "necessity of endurance" and begins to read a movie star magazine. The image this scene creates—Marian's dome covered head juxtaposed to the "Develop Your Bust" ad on the back cover of the magazine—provides what is perhaps Atwood's most biting commentary on the unrealistic expectations that are imposed on women and that are, as this chapter demonstrates, so difficult to combat.

When the process is finally complete, Marian is not pleased with the finished product. She considers asking the hairdresser to comb out some of the artificial "tusk-like spitcurls" but is intimidated by the "official surroundings and specialist implements." Telling herself that he must know what he is doing and that Peter will surely like it, she decides to leave her decorated head the way it is. Marian's passivity in this scene can be summed up by the description of another just a few pages later: she follows the crowd, impelled not by the sense of being able to control her own destiny but by some "herd- or lemming-instinct."

In Chapter 25, Marian is repeatedly represented as divided and torn. While taking a bath, for example, she sees herself reflected in the bathtub taps and spout—three self-reflections at once—and does not immediately recognize herself. She then notices a film of soap and dirt in the tub water and fears that she is dissolving, coming apart layer by layer. Seeking a quick source of comfort, Marian puts on her engagement ring. She hopes that it will act as a "protective talisman" and "keep her together." However, Marian's panic is not subdued by the ring. In fact, moments after putting it on, she starts to worry about that evening's party: she is afraid that she will lose her shape and be unable to contain herself. She also fears that she will begin to talk a lot—a comment that recalls her remark about Duncan's "liquid confessing." She thought Duncan's incessant talk at the laundromat "foolhardy" and compared it to "an uncooked egg deciding to come out of its shell." To her, confessing involves the risk of "spreading out too far [and] turning into a formless puddle." Her fear of breaking down and "tell[ing] everybody" suggests that there are certain things that she would like to keep to herself. It also suggests that there are certain things that she would prefer to keep from herself (she does not name what she fears telling).

Marian's attention then turns to the two dolls displayed on her dresser. She imagines that she is inside the dolls and that she can see herself, simultaneously, through the two pairs of eyes. Each doll sees something different and the two overlapping images appear to be drifting further and further away from each other. At the centre, the thing that holds them together "would soon be quite empty." The symbolic significance here is evident: as Marian continues to keep her true feelings from breaking out of her artificially constructed shell, and as she continues to adapt herself according to the whims of others, she is gradually losing sight of herself.

Marian's perception of authority can be understood, to a certain degree, by examining her relationship with her landlady. A single example—the feeling of obligation which drives Marian to clean the bathroom after Ainsley has taken a bath—is sufficient to demonstrate Marian's need to conform to the authority presiding over her own home. But the landlady's hypocritical facade comes tumbling down on the night of the party, and when it does, Marian is unable to "imagine why she had ever been even slightly afraid of her"—she and her empty beliefs "had been so easily deflated." By having this symbol of authority and supposed morality shattered by Ainsley's spontaneous defiance, Atwood appears to be setting the stage for the scenes to come. Individuals, as Ainsley earlier suggested and here demonstrates, can "lead the way" and make a difference.

Study Questions

1. Lying in bed with Peter on the day after Valentine's Day, Marian worries about her body's recent rejection of rice pudding. What else is Marian worried about?

2. Explain the jealousy Marian feels towards her friend Clara.

3. What does Marian give Peter for Valentine's Day? Why? When?

4. Does Peter like the gift? Does Marian?

5. Why does Marian choose to buy a red sequined dress that she does not really like?

6. Marian is not pleased with her new hair style but does not ask the hairdresser to change it. Why not?

7. Why is Marian afraid of losing her engagement ring?

8. What does Marian do when feeling herself dissolve in the tub?

9. Does this ease her panic?

10. What does she do next?

Answers

1. What bothers her, essentially, is the thought that she may not be normal. She is afraid to tell Peter about her problem because he might think that she is "some kind of freak" and postpone the wedding.

2. Marian envies Clara because whatever was going to happen to her had already happened. She does not want to change places with Clara; she simply wants to know what she is becoming.

3. Marian gives Peter a heart-shaped cake with pink icing. She buys it because he had sent her a dozen roses and she, having no gift for him, felt guilty. She buys the cake on the day after Valentine's Day.

4. Marian spits the cake out as soon as she tastes it; Peter does not notice anything wrong with the cake.

5. Marian goes shopping for a new dress because Peter suggested she might want to buy a dress that wasn't quite as "mousy" as the ones she already owned. She chooses that particular dress because the saleslady tells her that it suits her.

6. She is intimidated by the official surroundings and assumes that the stylist must know what he is doing. Also, she thinks that Peter will like it.

7. Because she knows that Peter would be furious—he is very fond of it.

8. She puts the engagement ring back on, seeing it as a "protective talisman that would help keep her together."

9. No. The panic is still with her as she climbs the stairs to her apartment. She feels unable to face the party and all of Peter's friends. She is afraid of losing her shape, of not being able to contain herself.

10. She calls Duncan.

Suggested Essay Topics

1. According to Clara, Marian will eventually get over her eating problems. Discuss the potential repercussions of this attitude.

2. Among the many foods that Marian is unable to eat is the cake she buys for Peter on the day after Valentine's Day. Discuss why this might be significant.

3. Marian thinks of her engagement ring as a "protective talisman" that will keep her together. However, it fails to ease her panic. Discuss.

Chapters 26-29

Summary

Because the elevator in Peter's building is not working, Marian and Peter must use the stairs to get to his seventh-floor apartment. As they reach the fifth-floor landing, Marian finally decides to tell Peter that she has invited some other friends to the party. During the car ride over, she had been wondering how she was going to tell him; she is unsure whether he will be happy or mad. Taking a step away from Peter, Marian grips the railing and tells him. Peter is only slightly irritated and is surprised to learn that Marian has so many friends that he does not know. He tells her that he will have to make a point of getting to know them to find out about her private life. Hearing this, Marian begins to panic and asks herself how she could have been so stupid as to invite all those people. She worries that Duncan might give her away or drop an insinuating remark. Peter, of course, would be furious: he would think that someone had infringed on his "private property rights." She tries to think of a way to stop them from coming.

Inside the apartment, Marian removes her overcoat and Peter puts his hands on her bare shoulders, kisses her lightly on the back of the neck, and says: "Yum yum." She takes her coat into the bedroom and, seeing her reflection in the mirror, is reminded of Peter's reaction when he came to pick her up. He told her that she looked

marvellous, implying that it would be greatly appreciated if she could manage to look like this all the time. Her attention is then diverted to the contents of Peter's closet. She stares at his collection of costumes hanging neatly in a row and realizes that she is observing them with resentment. She thinks they assert an "invisible silent authority." Marian then thinks that it is not resentment she feels but fear.

Marian goes into the kitchen to prepare food snacks for the guests. When she is almost done, Peter comes up behind her and half unzips her dress. He tells her it's too bad they haven't got time for a quick hop into bed but adds that he does not want to get her "all mussed up." Marian suddenly asks Peter if he loves her. In response, he kisses her on the earring and assures her that he does—especially in that red dress. A few moments later Peter calls Marian into the bedroom where he is fiddling with one of his cameras. He tells her that he would like to get a couple of shots of her alone before the guests arrive. The red, he says, will come out nicely on a slide. Marian hesitates and Peter directs her to lean up against the gun rack. Marian stands there stiffly while Peter points the lens at her and tells her to "look natural" and "stick out [her] chest." She wants to tell him not to touch the shutter-release but is unable to move. A knock at the door interrupts Peter before he can take a picture. As Peter leaves the room, Marian wonders what was wrong with her: "It's only a camera," she says.

The first to arrive at the party are the three office virgins, each of whom compliment Marian's dress and say that she should wear red more often. All three have come hoping that an eligible version of Peter will walk in through the front door and whisk them away. Marian wonders what their reaction will be when Duncan and his roommates show up—and what their reactions will be when they see the three office virgins. She imagines screams and a mass exodus, one threesome running out the door, the other leaping out the window. Peter's friends and their wives begin to arrive and the room divides into the standard territories: wives on the sofa, husbands near the hi-fi. Clara and Joe arrive and Marian is shocked to see that they have brought Len Slank with them. Marian hustles Clara into the bedroom and asks her what Len is doing here. Clara explains that he arrived at their door in very bad shape, telling a story about a woman he's been having trouble with. Marian worries that Len's presence might upset Ainsley enough to do something unstable.

Back in the living room Marian notices that Emmy, Millie, and Lucy have identified Len as single and available and have cornered him against a wall. His face shows "incredulity, boredom and alarm." Joe finds Marian and tells her how happy he is that she asked them to the party. Clara, he explains, has so few chances to get out of the house. He tells Marian that it's hard for women who have been to university because they get the idea that they have a mind. Then, when they get married, their "core gets invaded" thereby setting up a conflict with their feminine role which demands passivity. He wonders whether it would not be better if women did not go to university at all; that way they wouldn't end up feeling as though they've missed out on the life of the mind.

When Ainsley arrives Marian immediately warns her about Len. Ainsley assures her friend that she is not at all bothered by Len's presence. On her way to the kitchen, Marian notices that Lucy and Peter are in the bedroom. Marian figures that Lucy must have realized that hanging around Len was futile and finds it pathetic that she would instead try for Peter. He is, after all, "off the market." Peter sees Marian and waves his camera to her, saying that it is almost picture time. Marian returns to the living room just as Duncan and his roommates arrive. Marian opens the door and is met by Trevor's puzzled face: he does not recognize her. Fish and Duncan, along with another person, stand behind him. Marian reintroduces herself and invites them in. As the others pass through the doorway, Duncan grabs Marian's arm and pulls her into the hall. He looks at her for a moment, says he did not know the party was a masquerade and asks her who she is supposed to be. He then tells Marian that he does not want to go inside. But Marian, feeling that it is suddenly very important for him to come with her, tells him that he has to meet Peter. Duncan thinks that a bad idea: "One of us would be sure to evaporate," he says. Marian repeats her request but Duncan is already heading down the hall, on his way to the laundromat.

As she reenters the living room, Marian overhears Len tell Ainsley that she will never get him. Ainsley then smashes her glass on the floor, stopping all conversation, and announces that she and Len are going to have a baby. Marian sees that Ainsley is forcing the situation and worries that Len is going to hit her. Instead, he makes an announcement of his own. He says that the christening is going to take place right away—a "baptism in utero"—and pours his beer over Ainsley's head. At that moment Peter rushes in and snaps a photo, exclaiming that the party is "really getting off the ground." The first to approach and comfort Ainsley is Fish. He pulls off his sweater and begins to dry her off.

The party (minus Ainsley, Fish, and Len) continues and, after having another drink, Marian concludes that she is coping. She notices that Peter is still taking pictures and is reminded of home-movie ads in which the father uses roll after roll of film on ordinary events. She thinks that this is what he's turning into. The real Peter, she concludes, is nothing surprising or frightening, he is merely a bungalow, backyard cooking man. Still drinking, she begins to imagine what Peter will be like later in life. She imagines walking down a corridor and opening various doors to her future with Peter. Through the first door, she sees Peter at 45, standing beside a barbecue, wearing a chef's apron, and holding a long fork in one hand. She looks for herself but she is not there. She thinks this is the wrong room and decides to try another. As she walks towards it she sees that Peter is holding a cleaver in his other hand. The door brings her back to the party where everybody is now getting ready to leave. She sees herself as a "two dimensional figure" posing like "a paper woman in a mail order catalogue" and thinks that this could not be it, there has to be more. She runs to the next door. Peter is there, camera in hand, and there are no other doors. Marian reaches behind her to find the exit but Peter raises his camera and aims it at her, his mouth "open in a snarl of teeth." There is a blinding flash of light and Marian screams "No" and covers her face with her arm. When she looks up Peter is there asking what is wrong—it is the real Peter. She asks if that photo was of her but it was not—he promises to get to her later. He also tells her that she is swaying and that she shouldn't have any more to drink.

Marian realizes that she is still safe and that she must get out before it is too late. It all depends on getting as far as Duncan, she thinks. He would know what to do. She calls Duncan's number but

there is no answer. As she goes to the bedroom to get her coat, Peter calls her from the living room—he wants to take a group photo. Counting on her dress to act as camouflage, she heads for the front door and manages to slide out unseen. Immediately she begins to run, knowing that this time she cannot let Peter catch her. If he pulls that trigger she "would be stopped, fixed indissolubly in that gesture. . . unable to move or change." She runs through the snowy streets with the knowledge that Peter might be stalking her just as he stalked the guests in his living room. She thinks of him as an "intent marksman with an aiming eye" who has been hiding beneath his other layers—a "homicidal maniac with a lethal weapon in his hands." Finally, she looks behind her and sees that there is nobody there.

Marian finds Duncan sitting in the laundromat. He is smoking a cigarette and watching the washing machine in front of him. She tells him that she could not stay at the party any longer and that she just wanted to be with him. Duncan, however, tells her that it is her duty to go back to Peter. He also assures her that he himself requires no rescuing and suggests that maybe it is she who wants him to rescue her. Marian changes the subject and proposes that they go some place else. By this she means spending the night together. Duncan agrees and they decide to look for a room somewhere.

As they walk, Marian thinks about the party and whether Peter has noticed she is no longer there. Eventually, they find a shabby hotel that will rent them a room. Once inside, Marian wonders what she is doing there and what Peter would think if he knew. Duncan begins to fiddle with an ashtray and Marian decides that something has to be done. She orders him to put down the ashtray, take off his clothes, and get into bed. She prepares to join him but Duncan refuses to let her in until she peels all the junk off her face. Fornication is all very well in its way, he says, but he doesn't want to come out "looking like a piece of flowered wallpaper."

Half an hour later, Duncan announces that it is no use, he must be incorruptible. Marian kneels beside him in the bed while he has a cigarette. She is tense with impatience and fear. She thinks that to evoke some response from the seemingly passive surface that is Duncan is the most important thing she could do and she could not do it. This knowledge fills her with an icy desolation. Duncan then puts out his cigarette and tells her to lie down. He strokes her, straightening her out almost as if he is ironing, and tells her that "it isn't something you can dispense."

The next morning, Marian and Duncan sit in a grimy coffee-shop near the hotel. Marian is thinking about last night and how everything had seemed resolved: Peter's hunting eyes had been absorbed into some "white revelation" and she had found a simple clarity. Now, that clarity has faded and whatever decision she had made has been forgotten. She consoles herself by thinking that something has at least been accomplished in Duncan's life. However, she knows that for her, nothing is finished. She will have to see Peter and explain. Looking down at the breakfast menu, Marian feels something move in her throat. She tells Duncan that she cannot eat and realizes that it has finally happened: her body has completely cut itself off. To Duncan, Marian's inability to eat simply means that he can afford to order himself a bigger breakfast.

After breakfast, Marian is not yet ready to go back home and asks Duncan to stay with her a little while longer. They go for a walk and he leads her on a long trek to one of the many ravines that fissure the city. Marian, thankful that she is with someone who knows where he is going, gratefully allows herself to be led. As they approach the ravine, Duncan begins to run down a steep hill, dragging Marian behind him. She calls for him to stop but he keeps on running, telling her that they're escaping. They run past a danger sign and Marian fears that they will go hurtling over some unseen edge. Finally, Duncan announces that they have arrived. Marian is startled when she realizes that they are standing on the edge of a cliff. They sit for a moment on the edge overlooking a huge circular pit and then get up and lie in the snow. They discuss Marian's reluctance to return home and Duncan suggests that her problems might be in her mind. He tells her that although he himself lives in a world of fantasies, the fantasies are largely his own. She, on the other hand, doesn't seem to be happy with hers. Marian thinks that Duncan is possibly right but does not know how to get out of it. What she really wants, she realizes, is simple safety. She thought that she had been heading towards it but now sees that she hasn't gotten anywhere.

As their conversation continues, Marian discovers that last night had not been Duncan's first time like she thought. As a result, the nurse-like image of herself that she had been trying to preserve crumples. But after thinking about it for a few minutes she decides that it does not matter. She sits up, brushes the snow off her sleeves, and says that she must now decide what to do. Duncan offers no help; as far as he is concerned, she has invented her "own personal cul-de-sac" and will have to think her way out of it. Marian asks Duncan if he will come with her to speak to Peter but he refuses. He leads her back to the street and walks away.

Analysis

Ainsley has made it clear that she does not approve of Marian's decision to marry Peter. According to her, Marian does not know Peter well enough to marry him. At the beginning of Chapter 26, Ainsley's warnings appear to be justified. As they walk up the stairs to Peter's apartment, Marian frets as she tries to think of a way to tell Peter that she has invited some of her friends to the party. Not only does she fear Peter's reaction to this rather unalarming news, she fears it enough to feel the need to take a step back and grip the railing: "there was no telling what he might do." She thinks of Peter as an "unknown quantity" whose reactions she can no longer calculate in advance. One of the reasons she is reluctant to tell Peter about her last minute invitations is that she dreads the thought of facing his questions. If Peter finds out about her friendship with Duncan, he would, Marian thinks, be furious. He would think that someone had infringed on his "private property rights."

As they enter the apartment, Peter kisses Marian on the back of the neck and utters a playful "Yum yum": frosted in hair spray and sweetly scented, Marian has applied all the right ingredients to whet Peter's appetite. If he had his way, this is how Marian would look all the time. In other words, he would like her to be other than she actually is—the realization of an ideal image read about in murder mysteries or seen in photography magazines. When Marian later asks him if he loves her, he kisses one of her decorations (a borrowed earring) and assures her that he does, especially in that red dress. But Marian's view of herself differs greatly from Peter's. Looking at herself in his bedroom mirror, she notices that her arms, the only parts of her not covered by cloth, nylon, leather, or varnish, look fake and plastic. Wearing the bits and pieces of other people's jewelry, makeup, and taste in clothes, Marian is unable to see herself as whole. Her attention is then turned to Peter's clothes, hanging in his closet. Marian feels resentment, then fear, as she contemplates her future husband's costumes of authority.

A little while later, Marian becomes anxious when Peter expresses the wish to "get a few shots" of her before the guests arrive. Telling her that the "red ought to show up well on a slide," Peter directs Marian to lean up against his gun rack. The association between cameras and guns is made early in the novel—it was Peter's hunting story and the visual image created by his description of the photos taken to record the bloody mess that led to Marian's panic at the Park Plaza bar and to the ensuing hunt through city streets. Here, Peter's words evoke that story once again. The red in the hunting photos came from the rabbit's blood and guts that were, in Peter's words, "all over the place." Now, it is Marian who is covered in red and who is "backed against the wall," paralyzed in fear by the aiming lens. Of course, Peter is completely unaware of Marian's discomfort and, with a single breath, and without even a dash of irony, tells her "to stick out [her] chest, and. . . look natural." The image of the woman he wants to create is one that is, like the hunter's prey or the photographer's subject, under his control.

There are two very obvious examples of deliberate attempts to manipulate other people's behaviour in this chapter. In themselves, they appear harmless, but their significance in this novel demands attention. Earlier, Marian's behaviour was compared to that of a lemming. Here, Peter twice plans to shape his guests' actions by assuming that others are also driven by that same lemming instinct. Knowing, or at least hoping, that his guests will obediently follow the lead set by others, he and Marian leave their boots at the front door as "bait." Then, inside, Marian is told to put her coat on the bed. It will be a "decoy" for the other women's coats: "by it they would see where they were supposed to go." The most obvious association is, once again, to the girdle ad which baits women into believing that they must emulate the shape on display.

It is at the party that Marian finally realizes that she has to act. Already unrecognizable to herself, she proves unrecognizable to others too. Trevor stares at Marian blankly until she finally tells him who she is. Duncan, on the other hand, is not so much fooled by Marian's disguise as he is amused and repelled by it. He leaves, almost running, immediately after asking: "Who the hell are you supposed to be?" It is a seemingly simple question, yet one that Marian has neglected (or avoided) to ask (or examine) for too long. The pivotal word here is "supposed": by asking Marian this question, Duncan not only expresses his dislike for Marian's plastic appearance, he also raises the issue of expectations and obligations. Implied by his question is another question: who has the right to define that which is "supposed to be"?

Marian's first inclination is to run after Duncan, but feelings of obligation return her to the party. After a few drinks, she begins to contemplate her future life with Peter. She pictures him at 45 and is momentarily reassured by the image of a "normal" man with hobbies, working in the cellar and wearing blue jeans. She then imagines him wearing a chef's apron and standing beside a barbecue and is alarmed to see that the image does not include herself. *Recall Marian's visualization of Peter's hunting party in Chapter 8: she could not see the rabbit.* Looking more closely, Marian notices that Peter is holding a large cleaver in one hand. Still, there is no sign of herself. Has she disappeared? Dissolved? Been consumed?

When Marian's attention returns to the present, she sees herself as a "two-dimensional" figure, posing like a "paper woman in a mail-order catalogue." Convinced that there must be more than this, she returns to her visions of the future and stumbles into a room with no doors and where a raging Peter, "mouth opened in a snarl of teeth," takes aim at her with his camera. Significantly, it is when Marian discovers that Peter has not yet taken her picture that she realizes she is still safe and that she must get out before it is too late. As she leaves/runs away, Marian knows that, this time, she cannot allow Peter to catch her: "once that trigger is pulled she would be stopped, fixed indissolubly in that gesture. . . unable to move or change." Her image, captured and constructed by Peter, will have become permanent and real. She thinks of Peter as an "intent marksman with [an] aiming eye," a "homicidal maniac" with a lethal weapon. The lethal weapon is, of course, his camera and it is deadly because it renders her powerless. If photographed, it would be his version of her framed on the bookshelf of their future bedroom—the room that she now knows would look exactly like Peter's room does now. Her expression would be stifled, controlled, framed.

On the morning after her night with Duncan, Marian reveals that although she had, for a few brief moments, believed that "everything had seemed resolved," last night's "simple clarity" now eludes her. This letdown reveals to her that Duncan is not the answer to her problems. Significantly, it is on this morning that Marian's body, after a long period of mysterious fickleness, finally cuts itself off completely. Its long protest over her dependence on Peter reaches its peak when she transfers that dependence onto Duncan. Yet, Marian still feels unable to return home by herself and is reluctant to let Duncan go. He leads her on a wild journey through the city that ends on the edge of a cliff in one of the city's ravines. The location is significant: looking over the large circular pit, Marian becomes suspicious of the bottom and fears that it may break away. When Duncan points out the brickworks, explaining that it is pure clay, Marian thinks it wrong to have this "cavity in the city." She believed that the "ravine itself was supposed to be as far down as you could go." What Marian is realizing is that there is no foundation, no solid ground on which to build anything resembling certainty. It is here that Duncan asks her why it is she can't go back home. He suggests that her problems are all in her mind and admits that although he himself lives "in a world of fantasies," *his* fantasies are largely his own. Marian, on the other hand, does not seem happy with hers. The implication is that "her" fantasies are not really her own fantasies, but borrowed, internalized, and unchallenged fantasies built on and maintained by the belief in a reality resting on nothing more than clay. Similarly, the cul-de-sac that Marian must think her way out of is not entirely her own invention—the previous sections of this volume have shown that Marian has had lots of help making it seem real.

Study Questions

1. Describe Marian's feelings as she contemplates Peter's wardrobe closet.

2. What is Peter's response when Marian asks if he loves her?

3. Why is Joe so happy that he and Clara were invited to the party?

4. What is Trevor's reaction when Marian opens the door?

5. What is Duncan's reaction?

6. How does Peter react to Len's "baptism in utero"?

7. When Marian realizes that she is still safe, that Peter has not yet snapped her photo, she decides that she must get out before it's too late. Too late for what?

8. Where does Marian go when she leaves the party?

9. On the morning after their night together, what reason does Duncan give for not wanting to stay with Marian?

10. Why does Duncan discourage Marian from seeing a psychiatrist?

Answers

1. She feels that Peter's clothes assert an "invisible silent authority" and regards them with fear.

2. He kisses her on the earring and assures her that he loves her, especially in the red dress.

3. Because Clara never gets the chance to get out of the house.

4. Trevor does not recognize Marian. He then tells her that she should wear red more often.

5. Duncan examines Marian carefully and asks her who she is supposed to be.

6. He takes a picture.

7. By now a clear association has been established between cameras and guns. Marian has just imagined a rabid Peter aiming a raised camera at her and, as she runs away, thinks

that if he pulls the trigger (of his camera) and captures her on film, she would be stopped and "fixed indissolubly in that gesture." Her identity would be permanently defined.

8. Marian goes to the laundromat to look for Duncan.

9. He tells her that he's had enough "so-called" reality for now. He also tells her that she is no longer an escape and that if he stayed, he would feel obligated to start worrying about her.

10. Because a psychiatrist would only want to "adjust" her.

Suggested Essay Topics

1. Why is Marian so upset about Peter wanting to take a few pictures of her?

2. When Duncan sees Marian in her red party dress he asks her: "Who the hell are you supposed to be?" Does Marian know the answer to this question? Explain.

3. What finally causes Marian's body to cut itself off completely? Is there a simple answer to this question? Explain.

Chapters 30-31

Summary

Marian is not home for more than a few moments before she receives a call from Peter. He is angry and demands to know where she disappeared to last night. He tells her that she disrupted his evening and that he and Lucy drove up and down the streets look-ing for her. He also asks about the young man (Duncan) he heard about through Trevor. Marian offers a few vague answers but does not want to talk about this over the phone. Instead, she asks Peter to come over later in the day. She has not yet made any decisions and wishes to have some more time to think things over. What she wants, she decides, is a way of knowing "what was real," a test of some kind. She does not want to get tangled up in a discussion with Peter and tries to think of something that will allow her to avoid words. She begins to write out a grocery list but quickly puts down her pencil. All of a sudden, she knows "what she [needs] to get."

Marian goes to the supermarket and moves "methodically" up and down the aisles finding everything she needs. Not wanting to use anything that was already in the house, she buys eggs, flour, lemons, sugar, icing sugar, vanilla, salt, food colouring, and cocoa. When she gets home she bakes a sponge cake. Once it is mixed and in the oven, she makes and divides the icing. One portion she dyes bright pink, another chocolate brown, and a third she leaves white. As the cake cools Marian feels glad that Ainsley is not at home: she does not want her to interfere with what she is going to do.

Marian cools the cake by the open window and then begins "to operate." She divides the cake in two, using the first half to make a head and body and the second to add arms and legs. She sticks the whole cake together with the white icing. Eventually, she has a blank white body and quickly sets about clothing it. First, a bikini is added, then a dress with ruffles around the neck and hem. A smiling pink mouth and pink shoes are added next. With the chocolate icing Marian draws the eyes, nose, and lines demarcating the arms and legs. The hair is a mass of swirls and curls and the eyes are green with silver globular decorations acting as pupils.

Finally, the cake-woman is complete and looks like an elegant china figurine. Marian contemplates her creation and suddenly worries about what will become of it. Thinking that her cake looks very appetizing, Marian says: "You look delicious. . . And that's what will happen to you; that's what you get for being food." She feels sorry for her creature, powerless to do anything about it. Before long Marian hears Peter's footsteps on the stairs. She considers how infantile and undignified she will seem to a "rational observer" and decides that if Peter thinks her silly she will believe him and accept his version of herself.

When Peter enters the apartment, Marian tells him that she has a surprise for him. Although she is momentarily distracted by the thought that her fears and flight to Duncan had been little more than an evasion ("Peter was not the enemy after all. . . It was Duncan that was the mutation"), Marian goes to the kitchen and returns carrying the cake. She places it in front of Peter and says: "You've been trying to destroy me, haven't you. You've been trying

to assimilate me." She then tells him that she's made him a substitute—something he will like much better. Peter stares at the cake, then at Marian. She is not smiling. He leaves shortly afterwards without eating any of the cake. As a symbol, Marian thinks that her cake has failed. Suddenly, she is hungry and begins to eat some of the cake herself. Almost immediately, the part of her not occupied with eating begins to feel nostalgic for Peter. She imagines him: well dressed, scotch in hand, foot on the head of a stuffed lion, a revolver strapped to his body—"he would definitely succeed." When Marian is halfway through the legs, Ainsley arrives with Fish. Ainsley is surprised by the cake-woman and tells Marian that she is rejecting her femininity. Marian dismisses this comment as nonsense and stabs the cake with her fork, severing the head. "It's only a cake," she says.

In the final chapter, Marian resumes her first-person narration. Ainsley is gone and Marian is busy cleaning the apartment. Duncan calls wanting to know what happened, and Marian explains that she has realized Peter was trying to destroy her and that she is now looking for a new job. What Duncan wants to know, however, is what happened to Fish. Marian is a little irritated by this; now that she was thinking of herself in the "first person singular" again, she found her own situation more interesting than his. Duncan reminds her that it is her turn to be the sympathetic listener and she invites him to come over. When he arrives they sit together at the kitchen table and Marian tells him that Fish and Ainsley are married. Ainsley had come home yesterday to pack and announced that she and Fish were going to Niagara Falls for their honeymoon. She also said that Fish would be "a very good one" (father). Upon hearing these details, Duncan figures that he will now have to move out of his apartment and wonders what will become of him. Marian's thoughts turn to Len. The news of Ainsley's marriage had not relieved him; he is still living at Clara's and is afraid to leave the house.

Marian serves coffee and the two discuss her now-resolved eating problem (she is eating again). Marian believes that Peter was trying to destroy her but Duncan argues that this is just something she made up. He tells her that it was actually she who was trying to destroy Peter. But the real truth, Duncan says, is that he (Duncan)

was trying to destroy her. Or that he was trying to destroy Peter, or they each other. Finally, Duncan dismisses these accusations and says that she is "back to so-called reality"—she is "a consumer." Marian offers Duncan some of her cake, as she still has the torso and head left. She brings him a fork and the remains of the cadaver and then watches as the cake disappears. It gives her a peculiar sense of satisfaction to see him eat it, as if her work "hadn't been wasted after all." Duncan finishes the last chocolate curl and says thank you: "It was delicious."

Analysis

When Peter finally reaches Marian on the phone the day after the party, she feels as though she is on the threshold of a decision and asks him to come over later in the day. What she needs, she thinks, is a test. Almost instinctively, she decides what she needs to do and what she needs to get. Recently, Marian's dependency on the opinions and thoughts of others has distorted her ability to make decisions based on her own true beliefs and feelings. Her decision to quit her job after the wedding is one such example. Another is her belief that she went to the beauty salon of "her own free will." It is true that she was not carried or forcibly pushed into the salon, but whose will was she actually obeying when she made the decision to go? Her quick decision here demonstrates that Marian is once again trusting her own instincts and judgement. At the supermarket, she moves "methodically" through the aisles, carefully choosing her ingredients. As she does so, "her image [begins to take] shape." Also taking shape is the substitute self Marian is planning to offer Peter. A soon-to-be sponge cake, the ingredients in Marian's shopping cart are already beginning to soak up Marian's decorous and removable layers.

Once the cake is cooled, Marian begins "to operate," scooping and moulding the cake into her cake-woman. The language here recalls that used when Marian herself was being decorated and operated on in the beauty salon. Now, the roles have been reversed and it is Marian who is doing the operating, creating instead of being (re)created. The cake is decorated with pink ruffles and a smiling pink mouth—also reminiscent of Marian's experience at the beauty salon (the salon reeked of pink). When she is done,

Marian's creation looks like a china doll. Vacant looking and possessing only a "glitter of intelligence," Marian's cake is the perfect (and completely edible) representation of society's perfect woman. Appropriately, Marian begins to worry about what will happen to her cake now that it is complete (decorated). She gives it fair warning about what kind of treatment it can expect to receive, telling it: "You look delicious" and "That's what you get for being food." As a representation of the ideal woman, Marian is aware that its fate lies in the hands (and mouths) of others.

Despite the assertiveness Marian displays while preparing the cake, she falters somewhat when she hears Peter's footsteps on the stairs. She imagines how silly she will look to a "rational observer" and worries that if Peter finds her silly, she will believe his version of herself. Peter arrives in his usual suit and tie—his costume of authority—and Marian slips a little when she sees him. She then remembers what it is she wants to accomplish with her cake. Unlike the first cake-test, which was given to Peter with the hope of proving herself normal, the cake Marian creates here is offered with the intent of debunking that very same notion of "normal." Faced with Marian's substitute—the reproduced image of the ideal nonexistent woman that he's wanted all along—Peter is rendered silent and harmless. And whereas, in earlier scenes, it was Marian who felt threatened by Peter, now it is Peter's eyes that widen "in alarm." By appropriating this symbol of her own powerlessness, Marian assumes control of her own fate. She is now able to define Peter the way he attempted to define her—by imagining him fixed in the image of a photo: posed in a posh salon, impeccably dressed, a scotch in one hand, a revolver strapped beneath one arm, a foot on the head of a stuffed lion, and a thumbtack just above his left ear.

When Ainsley arrives and finds Marian eating her cake-woman, she tries to "gulp down the full implication of what she [sees]" and tells her roommate that she is "rejecting [her] femininity." Marian, of course, now knows that this is nonsense and announces that "it's only a cake." Ironically, Ainsley has suddenly embraced the very notion of femininity that Marian has recently rejected. Once decidedly anti-marriage, wishing to avoid a husband at all costs, Ainsley has now caught herself a man (Fish) and is off to that most predictable of honeymoon destinations, Niagara Falls.

The final chapter begins with a long-absent "I." Her engagement to Peter now off, Marian regains control of her own narrative. She is also eating again. Duncan, however, is unconvinced by Marian's analysis of her situation. He claims that her belief that Peter was trying to destroy her is "just something [she] made up." When he then suggests that it was, in fact, she who was trying to destroy Peter, Marian experiences a "sinking feeling" that can only be interpreted as self-doubt. Also troubling is Duncan's final summation of Marian's ordeal: he tells her that she is "back to so-called reality"—a "consumer." With Marian now looking for a new job, a new home, and presumably a new boyfriend, one cannot help but wonder if anything has really changed.

Atwood has described *The Edible Woman* as a "circle" and as "more pessimistic than [her second novel] *Surfacing*" because in that novel, "the heroine. . . does not end where she began" (Sandler, 1981). However, Marian has, thanks to the experiences of the past few months, learned much about herself and about what she wants to do and who she wants to be. She successfully removes herself from a relationship that allowed her no room for self-expression and from a job that provided her with no source of satisfaction. She has also developed a new awareness of self and of others and will certainly be better prepared to handle similar trials in the future. *The Edible Woman* does not end with the traditional marriage between the heroine and her lucky suitor, but does this simply mean that Marian ends where she began? Is the ending truly circular? Is the novel ultimately optimistic or pessimistic? The task of making any final conclusions is left to Atwood's readers.

Study Questions

1. Why does Marian bake a cake shaped like a woman?

2. What does she hope to accomplish by presenting Peter with a substitute woman?

3. When Marian completes her cake, she feels a certain pity for it. Why?

4. Is there any evidence that Marian is still not completely sure of herself?

5. What does Ainsley think of Marian's cake-woman?

6. What is to be made of Marian's statement, "Now that I was thinking of myself in the first person singular again. . ."

7. Does Ainsley find a father image for her baby?

8. What does Duncan think of Marian's explanations for breaking off her engagement to Peter?

9. How does Duncan interpret Marian's new-found ability to eat?

10. Who severs the cake's head from its body?

Answers

1. The simplest answer to this question is that Marian wishes to present Peter with a test.

2. Marian accuses Peter of trying to assimilate her. By presenting him with this substitute cake-woman, she hopes to reclaim her right to determine her own identity and reject the version of herself that he has been trying to create.

3. Marian feels powerless: the fate of the cake, which looks delicious and very appetizing, has been decided.

4. She believes that her actions will appear infantile to a rational observer. She also thinks that if Peter finds her silly she will accept his version of herself.

5. She thinks that Marian is rejecting her femininity.

6. Marian has regained control of her own narrative, her own identity.

7. Yes, she marries Fish, Duncan's roommate.

8. He thinks the idea that Peter was trying to destroy her is just something she made up.

9. He tells her that she is back to "so-called reality"—she is a "consumer."

10. Marian severs the cake's head from its body.

Suggested Essay Topics

1. Near the end of the novel, Marian presents Peter with a cake
    that she has shaped into the likeness of a woman and ac-
    cuses him of trying to assimilate her. What is Marian trying
    to accomplish? What is Peter's reaction? Discuss.

2. Marian resumes her first-person narrative in the final chap-
    ter of the novel. Is this significant? Does this support or con-
    tradict Atwood's description of the novel as "circular"?
    Explain.

Sample Analytical Paper Topics

Topic #1

Near the beginning of *The Edible Woman*, Marian McAlpin asks: "What. . . could I expect to turn into at Seymour Surveys?" What could Marian turn into? What does she turn into? Has she changed by the end of the novel? If so, how has she changed, and why?

Outline:

I. Thesis Statement: *In* The Edible Woman, *Marian McAlpin escapes the tediousness of her job and the dangers posed by a life with her monopolizing boyfriend, Peter, and discovers her own identity.*

II. Ways in which Marian is prevented from finding an identity of her own:

    A. Menial job in a male-dominated business.

    B. Monopolizing boyfriend/fiancé.

    C. Susceptibility to the expectations of others.

    D. Compliance/passivity.

III. Ways in which Marian breaks the compliance cycle:

    A. The influence of aimless, nontraditional Duncan.

    B. Her eating problem: a sign that something is wrong.

    C. Visions of her future with Peter.

D. The realization that she has to do something—she's invented her own little cul-de-sac, must find her way out.

E. Bakes a cake and confronts Peter.

IV. Conclusion: By finally becoming aware of the external forces influencing her life, Marian is able to confront her own "fantasies" and live life on her own terms.

Topic #2

What is Marian's relationship to the other characters in the novel? How do her relationships with each of the characters influence the choices that she makes?

Outline:

I. Thesis Statement: *In* The Edible Woman, *Marian is surrounded by a cast of characters who represent a menu of possible futures. Throughout the entire period of her engagement to Peter, Marian struggles to make sense of these unappealing options until finally deciding to invent a new choice of her own.*

II. The cast of characters (as seen by Marian):

A. Ainsley: independent, deceptive, anti-marriage, gets married.

B. Clara: at one time, the "ideal of translucent perfume-advertisement femininity," now trapped and vegetative.

C. Peter: conservative, bound to be successful, controlling, destructive.

D. The three office virgins: interchangeable, waiting to be rescued by a man.

E. Duncan: Peter's opposite, acts as a guide to Marian, but not the victorious suitor.

III. Signs that Marian wishes to break away from the options that are presented to her:

A. She runs away from Peter (after leaving the bar, hides under Len's bed, runs away from Len's apartment).

    B.   Shift in narrative voice; a sign that all is not right.

    C.   Seeks comfort from/is drawn to Duncan.

    D.   Wishes to run through the freshly fallen snow and make new tracks of her own.

    E.   At the party, where all of these characters are assembled together, Marian decides that she must get away (her flight to Duncan proves disillusioning and ineffective).

    F.   Creates a substitute for the version of herself Peter wanted her to be/confronts Peter.

IV.   Conclusion: By the end of the novel, Marian has realized that the options presented to her are restrictive and destructive to her sense of individual identity. She creates a new beginning for herself by breaking ties with Peter and (quite literally) carving up his image of her.

Topic #3

At the end of the novel, Duncan tells Marian that she is back to "so-called reality"—a "consumer." This statement might suggest that Marian is no better off now than she was at the beginning of the novel. Construct an argument that demonstrates how Marian does not successfully escape society's mould.

Outline:

I.   Thesis Statement: *Although Marian appears to learn a great deal from the experiences of the past few months, the final chapters of* The Edible Woman *prove that she is still unable to free herself of external demands and expectations.*

II.   Evidence that Marian continuously lets others dictate her actions:

    A.   Agrees to work on a Saturday to conduct the Moose Beer survey.

    B.   Agrees to join Peter in the bathtub—even though she would clearly prefer the bed.

    C.   Agrees to a drastic make-over for Peter's party.

D.   Regularly second-guesses her own judgement.

E.   Her awareness of the manipulative intentions underlying supermarket music does not make her immune to it.

F.   Her decisions are often short-lived (for example, just moments before agreeing to marry Peter, she had decided that they were no longer involved).

III.   Evidence that Marian has not changed by the end of the novel:

A.   After her big decision in the ravine, Marian is still reluctant to return home by herself.

B.   After baking her cake, she experiences a moment of doubt and fears that she may still accept Peter's version of herself.

C.   After explaining to Duncan how she overcame her eating problems, Marian questions her own conclusions (because he disagrees with her).

D.   Marian is willingly returning to the same conditions and same expectations as the ones she has just escaped.

IV.   Conclusion: Although Marian does break off her engagement to Peter, there is no escaping the truth of Duncan's words: Marian will return to the world of consumerism and will continue to be a victim of its manipulations and injustices.

SECTION FOUR

Bibliography

Quotations from *The Edible Woman* are taken from the following edition:

Atwood, Margaret. *The Edible Woman*. First published 1969. Toronto: McClelland & Stewart, 1989.

Other works consulted:

Atwood, Margaret. "Great Unexpectations: An Autobiographical Foreword," *Margaret Atwood: Visions and Forms*. Kathryn VanSpanckeren and Jan Garden Castro, eds. Carbondale: So. Illinois UP, 1988.

Cameron, Elspeth. "Famininity, or Parody of Autonomy: Anorexia Nervosa and *The Edible Woman*," *Journal of Canadian Studies*, Vol. 20, No. 2 (Summer 1985): 45-69.

Carrington, Ildiko de Papp. *Margaret Atwood and Her Works*, Toronto: ECW Press, 1985.

Davey, Frank. "An Unneeded Biography," *Margaret Atwood: A Feminist Poetics*, Vancouver: Talon Books, 1984.

Harkness, David L. "Alice in Toronto: The Carrollian Intertext in *The Edible Woman*," *Essays on Canadian Writing*, Vol. 37 (Spring 1989): 103-111.

Sandler, Linda. in Catherine McLay's "The Dark Voyage: The *Edible Woman* as Romance," *The Art of Margaret Atwood: Essays in Criticism*. Arnold E. Davidson and Cathy N. Davidson, eds. Toronto: Anansi, 1981.

VanSpanckeren, Kathryn, and Jan Garden Castro, eds. "A Margaret Atwood Chronology," *Margaret Atwood: Visions and Forms*. Carbondale: So. Illinois UP, 1988.

Available at your local bookstore or order directly from us by sending in coupon below.